QUODLIBETS,

LATELY COME OVER FROM NEW BRITANIOLA, OLD NEWFOUNDLAND.

By
Robert Hayman

Adapted and Introduced by
David Reynolds

QUODLIBETS,

LATELY COME OVER FROM NEW BRITANIOLA, OLD NEWFOUNDLAND.

ISBN-13: 978-0986902727

Published by Problematic Press.

For more copies of this book, please visit: http://problematicpress.wordpress.com

Printed in the United States.

David Reynolds dedicates this adaptation of
Robert Hayman's *Quodlibets*
to his Mother and Father.

With love. Thanks.

Table of Contents

INTRODUCTION

By

David Reynolds

Poetry is cool. That's right. Poetry is cool, even if most people don't care for it these days. Many of us may love music and lyrics, singing along to our favourite tunes, but when it comes to appreciating poetry, it's clear that it's just not everyone's cup of tea. Sure, poets still write. There are writers' circles, there are sub-genres and niches, and there are those of us who enjoy their works, but poetry as a whole doesn't garner much attention anymore from a general audience. With this adaptation of Robert Hayman's *Quodlibets, Lately Come Over From New Britaniola, Old Newfoundland*, I hope to help change that.

Hayman was a prominent Englishman who served as the governor of England's colony in Newfoundland from 1618 to 1628. While presiding over the colony from Harbour Grace, Hayman penned this tremendous collection of epigrams called *Quodlibets.* It is entirely likely that his is the first substantial work of English poetry written in North America. And, it was made right here in Newfoundland.

Born in 1575 in Walborough, Devon, England, Hayman later graduated from Exeter College, Oxford University, and he led a rather successful political life in Totnes. No doubt, his political aspirations led him to the opportunity to serve as governor over the colony in this Newfoundland. In his lifetime he was known well as an explorer, a politician, and a poet. Shortly after returning to Europe, Hayman had his *Quodlibets* published. The book pleads with its audience, enticing the adventurous to settle in Newfoundland. Hayman perished in 1629, succumbing to complications from an infection during another of his expeditions, this time in Guyana.

Quodlibets is important not only because of its history but because of its quality. Hayman applied his craft studiously, and yet it still expresses his sentiments with outright glee or excruciating wit. Epigrams are clever ideas expressed in a pithy manner. Oftentimes, epigrammatists communicate their thoughts as brief satirical poems. Hayman's collection of epigrams aptly suits this definition. The title of Hayman's collection is a Latin word and, loosely translated, it means "what pleases." However, a quodlibet can also refer to a sly argument, frequently one involving a religious conceit. As such, many of Hayman's witticisms dwell on faith and the church. This is one of the more prominent themes found throughout Hayman's *Quodlibets*.

It becomes quite clear upon reading that Hayman tends to favour Protestant values; a fair number of his poems critique the Catholic church and the Pope of his era. While I personally do not endorse such opinions, they are nevertheless valuable to consider in the context of Newfoundland's colonial history. Other common themes that capture the poet's attention include appreciation of Newfoundland's rugged landscape, praise for the fair women of Newfoundland, and condemnation for sluts and sleveens. Of course, a sense of satire remains constant in each of these, leaving matters open for interpretation.

This adaptation of Hayman's *Quodlibets* is necessary so that a modern audience can easily read and comprehend his work. The English of the early 17th century is rather different from contemporary standards. In adapting Hayman's *Quodlibets* I have taken every effort to maintain the poetic character of the original text. The primary alterations concern adjusting spelling conventions.

Written in what is termed Early Modern English, the original text is replete with leftovers from Late Middle English. This style of English can be quite jarring for today's readers, likely turning many away from such a rich work. Imagine a modern reader endlessly encountering words like *wee*, *doe*, *ivstice*, or *theeues*. Some words readers can determine relatively easily, like *we* and *do*, but words like *justice* and *thieves* can be more difficult to recognize. When the entire text is written thusly, it can really kill the intellectual libido of a modern reader seeking pleasure. Ultimately, with obsolete spellings of words that can confound most modern readers, it was a shame such a barrier had prevented modern fans of poetry from enjoying Hayman's *Quodliebts.*

This adaptation addresses that concern, updating the language to be comparable with most modern editions of Shakespeare's works. Hence, the language can be understood more readily by readers today, yet it maintains the lyrical flavour and character of the verse.

Please, read and enjoy!

QUODLIBETS,

LATELY COME OVER FROM NEW BRITANIOLA, OLD NEWFOUNDLAND.

Epigrams and other small parcels, both Moral and Divine.

The first four Books being the Author's own: the rest translated out of that Excellent Epigrammatist, Mr. John Owen, and other rare Authors.

With two Epistles of that excellently witty Doctor Francis Rablais: Translated out of his French at large.

All of them
Composed and done at Harbour-Grace in Britaniola, anciently called Newfound-land.

By R. Hayman
Sometime Governor of the Plantation there.

LONDON,
Printed by Elizabeth, All-de,
for Roger Michell,
dwelling in Paul's Church-yard,
at the sign of the Bulls-head. 1628.

To the King's most Excellent Majesty, CHARLES, by God's especial mercy, King of Great Britain, France, and Ireland etc. Emperor of South, and North Virginia, King of Britaniola, or Newfound-land, and the Isles adjacent, Father, Favourer, and Furtherer of all his loyal Subjects right Honourable and worthy Plantations.

MAY it please your most Excellent Majesty, this last right worthy attribute of yours (no way insinuated, but justly affixed to your more ancient style) persuades these unworthy papers to presume (with your gracious leave and permission) to take the hardiness to kiss your sacred hands; hoping of the like success, that some unripe ears of corn, brought by me from the cold Country of Newfound- land, received from some honest, well- minded lovers of that action when they saw them: who with much- affected joy often beholding them, took much comfort in what they saw: but more, when they supposed it might be bettered, by industry, care, and honesty. These few bad unripe Rimes of mine (coming from thence) are in all humility presented with the like intendiment to your Majesty, to testify that the Air there is not so dull, or malevolent, but that if better wits were transplanted thither, neither the Summer's heat would dilate them, nor the Winter's cold benumb them, but that they might in full vigour flourish to good purpose. For if I now grown dull and aged, could do somewhat, what will not sharper, younger, freer inventions perform there? They would not walk as I here do, with short turns, leaning sometimes on others' inventions, skipping weakly from bough to bough; but with large walks, with long, and strong flights. I suppose it not fit at this time (but attending the success of this presumption) in some other larger manner to make known unto your Majesty, the inestimable riches of the Seas circling that land: The hopeful improvements of the main Land thereof: The more than probable, invaluable hidden treasures therein: The infinite abundance of combustible fiery materials fit for such an employment. It is only the Air at this time I desire to dignify, and that which is within that Horizon: Yet is my proof rather in hope of others, then in any actuated performance of mine own. If your Majesty will be pleased to give credit to your meanest subject, I may engage myself on this asseveration, That not only in this unprofitable (though not unpleasant)

Art, better wits would thrive there: but all other solid learning would walk uprightly without convulsions. I cannot but know how almost all your Royal hours are taken up in most Real, serious, solid employments: did I therefore imagine, that either your Majesty could, or graciously would vouchsafe the reading of these; they would be found some mine own, the rest, Translations. Mean and unworthy though they are, yet because some of them were born, and the rest did first speak English, in that Land whereof your gracious Majesty is the right, and lawful Sovereign, and King, by ancient descent and primary possession, and being the first fruits of this kind, that ever visited this Land, out of that Dominion of yours; I thought it my duty, to present and to prostrate these with myself at your Royal feet: For what I have mistakingly offended herein, or shall hereafter, I humbly beseech your Majesty's gracious, merciful, general, indulgence and pardon, unfeignedly beseeching God to bless your Majesty with abundance of all Earthly and Heavenly blessings. And that you may see an happy success of all your Foreign Plantations, especially of that of Newfound-land, I remain

Your Majesty's well meaning
and loyal Subject,

ROBERT HAYMAN.

My humble Muse, desires
likewise to kiss your sacred hands.

Fair, Bright, Illustrious Day-star of our times!
Cast a fair aspect on my short breath'd Rhymes:
If these to kiss your hands, are found unmeet,
I throw myself down at your Royal feet.

Humbly kisseth your
sacred hands, the
short-breath'd Muse of

ROBERT HAYMAN.

To my dear Friend and Fellow-Planter, Master Robert Hayman, *who with Pen and Person prepares more room for Christians in the Newfound-World.*

Whilst worldlings most build Castles in the Air,
Nibbling on baits, like *Orpheus* and *Senis* heir:
You spend your time both with your Muse and hand,
To edify our hopeful *Newfound-Land.*
To tame the rude, doth argue a brave spirit:
But to save souls, are works of greatest merit.
To plant and fish, from sloth you those persuade:
From errors these, to a more heavenly trade.
Thus whil'st but dorse some raking slaves engross,
You dig new grounds, and root up Trees and Moss.
You show the means to cut off suits and strife;
Means for good mean, to lead a pleasant life.
You search the Seas, and anchor with strong cables:
Which deeds you build on faith, as those on Babels.
Thus he who borrowed twice sweet *Orpheus* name;
Poor Cambriol's Lord, adds to your rising fame.

Your true friend
William Vaughan.

To the Facetious Epigrammatist, my loving Kinsman, Mr. Robert Hayman, *who composed these quaint* Quodlibets *at* Harbour-Grace, *in* Newfound-Land.

Your modest lines begot in *Harbour-Grace,*
Do *grace* that Harbour in old *Newfound-Land,*
Your witty lines the Muses do embrace.
Pernassus Nymphs admiring, mutely stand,
Seeing such sweet flowers from that barren soil;
As your neat *Quodlibets* which there did spring,
To *Omens* Genius you have given the soil.
By your sweet Epigrams, you there did sing.
I would you had the grace with our great King,
To do there your desires: A greater thing.

Your loving Kinsman,
Richard Spicer.

To the Lovers of the Muses, upon these Quodlibets.

Why do so many fondly dote upon
Parnassus Tempe, and that *Helicon*
Renowned by the *Greeks?* why praise they so
The *Muses* haunting *Tiber, Thame,* and *Po;*
As if no other *Hill,* or *Grove,* or *Spring,*
Should yield such *Raptures,* as these forth did bring?
Behold, even from these uncouth shores, among
Unpeopled woods, and hills, these strains were sung:
And most of theirs they seem to parallel,
Who boast to drink of *Aganippe's* well.
Despair not therefore, you that love the Muses,
If any Tyrant, you, or yours abuses:
For these will follow you, and make you mirth,
Ev'n at the furthest Angles of the Earth,
And those contentments which at home ye lees,
They shall restore you among Beasts and Trees.
Yours, *George Wither.*

An Acrostic-Sonnet. To his learned and well-beloved friend, Mr.

R ecreated with sweet favours
O f thy various curious Labours,
B eautified with Arts trim Treasures,
E x'lent for Poetic-Measures;
R apt (I say) with so rare view,
T hanks (me thinks) at least, was due.

H ere, I found such fragrant flowers,
A s, best dressed *Uranias* Bowers;
Y ielding Scents and Sights admired,
M eet, the Muse's Brows t'have tired:
A s, They (then) are, thus grac'd by Thee,
N ever, may They, Grace, deny Thee.

Ad eundem: Per eundem.
If *Newfound-Land* yield such commodities,
I'd thither trade, for so rare Merchandise.
Yours, *John Vicars.*

Harm I bare not.

Upon this anagram of my name, and the device of the West-Indian Guane.

If some should meet this Beast upon the way,
Would not their hearts-blood thrill for great affray?
Yet the West-Indian that best knows his nature,
Says, there is not any more harmless Creature.
So though my line havc much deformity,
Their end mine Anagram shall verify.

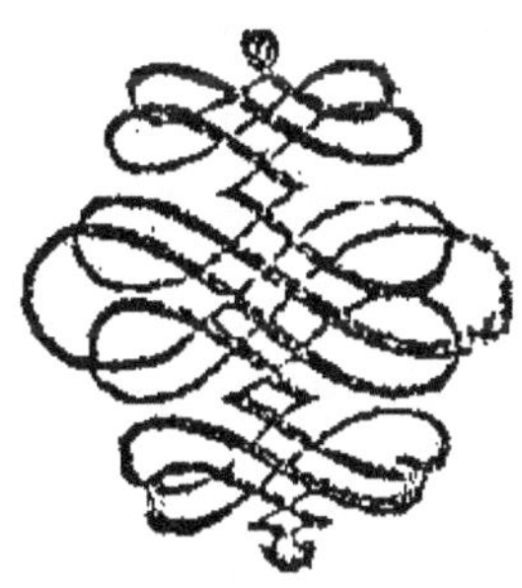

The First Book of *Quodlibets,* Done and Composed by the Author himself.

1. *Of mine own* Quodlibets.

Though my *best lines* no dainty things affords,
My worst have in them some thing else than words.

2. *To my Readers.*

I kept these closely by me some few years,
Restrained by my *knowledge,* and *my fears:*
I fear they are too shallow for the Schools,
I know they are too deep for shallow fools,
Yet there are many of a middle breeding
May think them good: nay richly worth the reading.

3. *To the perpetual renown of our learned King* JAMES, *King of* Great Britain, *etc. of famous memory.*

Wales, England, Scotland long did disagree,
Yet like a three-fold cord accord in Thee,
Such a cord hardly breaks, being wisely twist:
These three combined, may the whole world resist.

4. *Old* Lelius *to his wise friend* Scipio.

Let us sit down and by the fires light,
Let our discourse be without saucy spite,
We'll tell old toothless tales, which cannot bite,
Whilst young Fools to talk *Treason* take delight.

5. *Why God gives some Fools riches, and some wise men none.*

To a discreet friend.
Why fretst thou so, and art so fullen grown?
Thy neighbour Fool gets wealth, and thou getst none.
Wise, merciful, and just is God in it:
For he hath given him riches, and thee wit.
Alas poor Fool, if that he had no wealth,
He hath not wit to comfort his sad self.

6. *An old Apothecary made a new Doctor.*

He kill'd by others warrant formerly,
He kills now by his own authority.

7. *God doth all in all.*

It's held, The Stars govern the works of Men:
It's likewise held, Wisemen may govern them:
I hold, God overrules *Wise, Ways,* and *Stars:*
It's *He* that humbleth, and its *He* prefers.

8. *A worldly Man will have it by hook or by crook.*

If *wealth* I cannot *catch* with *Virtue's hook,*
I'll *haul* it to me, by my crafty *Crook.*

9. *Thrifty Charity, to a nameless Friend.*

On this Text thou dost seize, with griping hold,
Who gives the Poor, he shall receive fourfold.
This Text thou dost some pretty room afford,
Who gives the Poor, doth lend unto the Lord:
But this hard Text doth go against thy grain,
Give cheerfully, looking for nought again.

10. *Borrowing on Time, is worse then Bird-lime.*

As *Fowlers* use to take their *Fowl* with *Lime:*
So *Usurers* take borrowing *Fools* with *Time.*
Great danger 'tis, for *Birds, Bird-lime* to *touch.*
Not to keep *Touch* with *Usurers* it's as much.

11. *To a kind Fool.*

Oft into *Bonds* for others thou hast run,
But by those *Bonds,* thyself thou hast *undone.*
No Juggler ever show'd us such a cast,
To be *undone* by being bound so *fast.*
So Drunkards do with a like Juggling trick,
By gulping others healths, themselves make sick.

12. *Travelling in* England.

The travelling fashion of our Nation,
To pay without examination:
What our hard-rented Oasts may get thereby,
Is *Noble, Loose, Brave, Prodigality.*

13. *A persuasion to Humility.*

As when the *Moon* after the *Sun* doth go,
She daily doth, fairer, and fuller grow:
But when that *She* doth go before the *Sun,*
Her light grows less, and less, till she have none:
So whilst we follow *God* in humble fear,
His *Grace* in us, will beauteously appear:
But if we go before *God* in presumption,
His *Grace* in us will soon have a consumption.

14. *Why there are so few Hospitals built.*

If us hath *Will,* but wants good *Means* to do it.
Croesus hath *Means,* but wants a *Will* unto it.

15. *Lawyers profitable pastime.*

Lawyers do call *Plaintiff's Defence,* their *Plea:*
It rather might be called *Lawyer's Play.*

16. *The Policy of the Whore of* Babylon.

As common *Queens* have several quaint devices,
To hook all kind of men, by their entices:
So the spiritual *Whore* of *Babylon*
Hath several gins to entrap every one:
For *Villains, Wantons,* easy Indulgences:
For *Zealous, Wise,* Angelical pretences;
For *High-minds, Spenders,* honour she dispenses;
For *Women, Fools,* fine shows to please their senses.

17. *To Bald-pate.*

Though I want years, yet hoar I am through cares:
But *Whores* have made thy head white, without hairs.

18. *Worse than naught.*

Thou art not worthy of a *Satyr's* quill:
An *Epigram's* too short to show thine ill.

19. *Two filthy fashions.*

Of all fond fashions, that were worn by *Men,*
These two (I hope) will ne'er be worn again:
Great Codpieced Doublets, and great Codpieced britch,
At several times worn both by mean and rich:
These two had been, had they been worn together,
Like two *Fools,* pointing, mocking each the other.

20. *Fools are more masters of their wives than wise men. Scarce a Paradox.*

Wise men for shame mildly away will go,
Fools will stand stifly to't and have it so:
Wise men for quietness will sometimes yield.
Though *Fools* be beaten, they'll not quit the field.

22. *To a Pardon-Buyer.*

The *Pope* gives thee a sweeping Indulgence,
But thou must give him good store of thy pence:
So my *Lord Mayor* gives spoons all gilded o're,
Receives for each four or five pounds therefore.

22. *Worse than a Whore.*

Our common *Whores* turn *Roman Catholics,*
By that means they get Pardons for tricks:
These wandering Stars of common occupation,
Are rightly spher'd in this large Constellation:

I envy not that Church, that us so spites,
For fingering such notorious Proselytes.

23. *Why Kings speak in the Plural.*

Princes speak in the plural *Us,* and *We:*
It is their charge, from wrongs to keep *Us* free,
And *We* are wronged when *They* wronged be:
Thus *Plurals* with their *Plural* charge agree.

24. *The effects of God's Word.*

God's Word, to Sheep is grass; to Swine, hard stones;
Unto *Believers, Flesh;* to others, *Bones.*

25. *A Scottish Honest Man. A Londoner's Good Man.*

And Honest man, as *Scot'shmen* understand,
Is one, that mickle goods hath, at command.
A *Good man,* in the *Londoner's* account,
Is one, whose wealth to some Sum doth amount.
Lord, make me *Honest, Good* by thy instruction:
Then *Good* and *Honest* after their construction.

26. *How and whereof to jest.*

Jest fairly, freely: but exempt from it,
Men's misery, State business, Holy writ.

27. *The World's Whirligig.*

Plenty breeds *Pride; Pride, Envy, Envy, War,*
War, Poverty, Poverty, humble *Care.*
Humility breeds *Peace,* and *Peace* breeds *Plenty;*
Thus round this World doth roll alternately.

28. *On a Good fellow Papist, who makes no bones to eat Flesh on Fasting days.*

Thou holdst, thou saist, *the old Religion,*
Yet I know, the new *Diet* best likes thee.
That which thou call'st *the new opinion,*

I hold, yet the old *Diet* best likes me.

29. *Popery's Pedigree.*

Papistry is an old *Religion,*
Some part more old than *Circumcision,*
And some as ancient as are *Moses* Laws,
From whose Lies she some Ceremonies draws,
Which she will hold, by old *tradition.*
It is indeed a new *hodge-podgery,*
Of *Jewish* rites, elder Idolatry:
Of these old simples a new composition.

30. *The Married, to the Chaste.*

It would this World quickly depopulate,
If every one should die in your estate.

31. *The Chaste, to the Married.*

Therein you have the odds, herein we're even:
You fill the world, but we do people heaven.

32. *A Description of a Puritan, out of this part of the Litany, From Blindness of Heart, Pride, Vainglory, etc.*

Though *Puritans* the *Litany* deride,
Yet out of it they best may be descried:
They are *blind-hearted, Proud, Vain-glorious,*
Deep Hypocrites, Hateful and *Envious,*
Malicious, in a full high excess,
And full of all Uncharitableness.
A Prayer hereupon.
Since all tart *Puritans* are furnished thus,
From such false Knaves *(Good Lord deliver us.)*

33. *Love is betwixt Equals.*

Rich friends for rich friends, will ride, run and row,
Through dirt and dangers, cheerfully they'll go:
If poor friends come home to them, for a pleasure,

They cannot find the *Gentleman* at leisure.

34. *The difference betwixt good men and bad, is best seen after death.*

Good men like wax-lights blow'n out, favour well:
Bad men like tallow, leave a stinking smell.
Badmen's Fame may flame more while they have breath,
But *Good men's Name,* smell sweeter after death.

35. *To Sir Peirce Penniless.*

Though little coin thy purseless pocket line,
Yet with great company thou art ta'en up,
For often with Duke *Humfrey* thou dost dine,
And often with Sir *Thomas Gresham* sup.
The reward of Charity.

36. *To a rich Friend.*

Would'st thou be pitied after thou art dead?
Be pitifull whil'st thou thy life dost lead:
If whilst thou liv'st, the poor thou dost relieve,
Fearing the like supply for thee they'll grieve:
If now thou giv'st them nought, when thou art gone,
They will be glad, hoping for a new gown.
What have Foolish men to do with Prince's Secrets?

37. *Thought upon, on the preparation of a great Fleet, and may serve for all such actions hereafter.*

Fond men do wonder where this Fleet shall go:
I should more wonder, if that I should know.

38. *A Secret of State.*

Though *Peace* be lovelier, honourabler than War,
Yet warlike Kings most lov'd and honour'd are.

39. *Kings Paramount Subjection.*

What ways Kings walk, Subjects the same will go.
And many Kings, expect they should do so:
Therefore should Kings follow the *King Almighty:*
Kings are God's Subjects, if they govern rightly.

40. *Why Women are longer attiring of themselves than Men.*

Women 'tiring themselves have many lets,
Their *Fillets, Frontlets, Partlets,* and *Bracelets:*
Whilst down-right-neatless-plain men have but
one,
A Doublet double-let in putting on.

41. *Christ and Antichrist.*

Christ in the Temple shopboards overthrew,
Whipped thence the *buying and selling crew.*
The *Pope* in his *Church,* sets up his free *Fair,*
And whips all those, that will not buy his *Ware.*

42. *Wise men may be mistaken.*

Puritans ragged Reason of the rag of Popery, and
Papists
rotten Reason of thread-bare Antiquity.
Some too precise, will not some customs use,
Because that *Papists* did them once abuse:
As good a reason in sincerity,
As *Papists* oldness without verity.
Though these deserve to be hoist off the Schools,
Yet they are held by those that are no Fools.

43. *Unrighteous Mammon.*

Poets feigned *Pluto,* God of wealth, and *Hell:*
For they perceiv'd few got their *riches well.*

44. *A Dialogue betwixt a Wise King and a good Christian.*

The Wise King.
My neighbours secrets I desire to know,

That I their private plots may overthrow.

The good Christian.
I do neglect my Neighbour's words, and deeds,
I carefully survey mine own proceeds.

The Wise King.
If that my friends offer to do me harm,
I smite them first, and seek them to disarm.

The good Christian.
Though that my Foes do wrong me every hour,
I do them all the good lies in my power.

The Wise King.
By these and Justice, I shall wisely reign.
By this and faith, Heaven's Kingdom I shall gain.

45. *Sad-Men's lives are longer than Merry-Men's A Paradox.*

To him, whose heavy grief hath no allay
Of lightning comfort, three hours is a day:
But unto him, that hath his heart's content,
Friday is come, ere he thinks Tuesday spent.

46. *Popery's principal Absurdities.*

Of all the hood-winked tricks in *Popery,*
This is the lamentablest foppery:
When God is made to speak, and to command
Men, in a tongue they do not understand,
And Men commanded are to *Sing* and *Pray*
To such fond things that know not what they say,
And these men having madly, sadly pray'd,
Themselves do not know, what themselves have said.

47. *Of those who are too Kind, too Courteous, etc. Who overdo good things.*

Exuberant goodness, good men's names have stain'd,

Their too rank *Virtue* is by some disdain'd.
Yet 'tis not *Vice,* but *Virtue* over strain'd.

48. *Some Men's Testament is not their Will.*

He that will nothing spare whil'st he doth live,
And when he dies, unwillingly doth give,
Bequeathing what he gladly would keep still,
Makes a good Testament; but an ill Will.

49. *Why Wives can make no Wills.*

Men, dying make their *Wills:* why cannot Wives?
Because, Wives have their wills, during their lives.

50. *A just Retaliation.*

Dead Men bite not: great reason is there then,
That we which now do live, should not bite them.

51. *A Prayer.*

Lord, send me *Patience* and *Humility,*
And then send *Plenty,* or *Adversity:*
So if I be observ'd, or disrespected,
I shall not be puffed up, nor yet dejected.

52. *Reverent Grave Preachers.*

On holy days, I would hear such a Man,
Grave, holy, full of good instruction.

53. *Neat, quaint, nimble Pulpit Wits.*

These nimble Lads are fit for working days,
Their witty Sermons may keep some from plays.

54. *Divers complexions, and divers Conditions.*

A quiet, chaste mind, in flesh fair, and neat,
Is like to dainty sauce, and dainty meat.
A handsome body, with a mind debossed,
Is like to dainty meat sluttishly sauced.
A good wise mind, in flesh ill-favoured.

Is coarse meat, sweetly faust, well-savoured.
A froward, lewd mind in an ill shaped feat,
Is scurvy-scurvy sauce, and scurvy meat.

55. *Our Births, and Deaths, Rejoicing, and Mourning.*

When we are born, our friends rejoice, we cry:
But we rejoice, our friends mourn when we die.

56. *The Vanity of a Papistical Shift.*

You say you worship not the wood, nor stone,
For that's but the representation.
Wise Heathen us'd this *Fine Distinction.*
Millions that know not this subtlety,
Commit plain, palpable *Idolatry.*
Which you in them, do take some pains to breed,
That on their offerings you may fatly feed:
Why cause you else your *Saints* to weep, sweat, bleed?

57. *Curious barely Brethren.*

Those that will have all Names out of *God's* book,
And hold all other Names in detestation:
Poor begging *Lazarus* Name, these never took,
They more fear poverty, than *Profanation.*

58. *A Scrivener on a Trotter.*

Scriveners get most by riding trotting horses,
Copper-Arts, and Gall, for Ink towards their losses.

59. *Women's wise Tears.*

Disburthening tears breeds sad hearts some relief,
And that's one cause, few Women die of grief.

60. *To my Reader.*

If brevity my *Reader* do displease,
I use it more for his, than for my ease.

62. *Youths conceit, and Ages knowledge.*

I thought myself wise when I was at *School,*
But now I know, I was, and am a *Fool.*

63. *Hearbe-grace commonly called Rewe.*

Chaste men with name of *Hearbe of Grace* this grac't,
Because thereby, they thought they were kept chaste.
Some women hereupon did name it *Rewe,*
Because thereby they thought they lost their *Due.*

64. *To Writers of Heretical, and Keepers of false Books.*

When ye before God's Judgement Seat shall come,
Out of your own books, ye shall read your doom:
God need not to produce his own *True Book,*
For He doth daily on your *False books* look.

65. *To a Periwiggian, who hopes to gain by some friend's death.*

Thou maist well hope to be some dead-man's heir,
For thou already wear'st some dead-men's hair.

66. *Gossips and Good-wives.*

Whither go these *Good wives* so neat and trim?
They go a sipping, or a gossipping.
Come hither, *Boy,* wipe clean my Spectacles,
I shall see none of these *Good-women* else.

67. *A young Saint, and old Devil, to a Courteous old Man.*

Thou changed art of late (as I am told)
Less charitable grown, as thou grow'st old;
Thy former good was heat of youth in thee,
For grace once rooted, will grow like a Tree,
Which never can eradicated be.

68. *A mad Wench's Justice.*

Since not to be thy wives head thou do'st scorn,

Think this as just, *The head must wear the Horn.*

69. *We are God's Husbandry, or God's crop out of a fertile Christian Soul.*

A good Soul dressed with *Zeal,* plow'd up with fear,
Water'd with God's grace, a large crop will bear,
The root firm *Faith, Hope,* the blade spreading fair,
From these springs *Love,* into a large full ear:
The root is sure, the blade endures the storm,
With sheaves of *Love* we must fill full *God's* Barn.

70. *To a fair Whore.*

When we do see a *woman* sweetly fair,
We say that *God* hath done his part in her,
Thou passing *fair,* but passing *wicked art,*
In thee therefore *Satan* hath play'd his part.

71. *Riches is now a days the House upon Men's heads.*

In elder times good *Manners* made a *Man:*
In our wise age, good *Manors* maketh one.

72. *Money's Etymology.*

Many that's *Money:* for when I have none,
I pensive am, and sad, and sigh, and moan.

73. *The Treasure of the Church, or the Pope's Exchequer.*

Were't not for the huge, large, imagin'd chest,
The *Key* whereof hangs at the *Pope's* own breast,
Where over-doers' works, are rang'd for buyers,
For profane *Traitors, Gripers, Leachers, Liars,*
The *Popes* strong-bard-chest would be lin'd but thin,
A bag would serve to keep his treasure in.

74. *A wicked, contentious man's Epitaph.*

None living lov'd him, for his death none griev'd,
Save some say, Grief it was he so long liv'd.

75. *An Epitaph.*

On every well meaning man undone by his kindness.
My rich heart made me Poor, comforting Sad,
My helping, Impotent, my Goodness Bad.

76. *To one of Fortune's white Sons.*

Thou hast liv'd many years in perfect health,
Great friends thou hast, for thou hast got much wealth,
All things fall pat with thee, which thou would'st have,
Were it not pity thou should'st be a Knave?

77. *Death, and War.*

War begets *Famine,* famine, *Plague,* plague *Death,*
War breathes forth woes, but Death stops all woes breath,
War is great *A* of ills, and Death is *Z,*
In war's red Letters, Death's feast-days are read.

78. *The Popish Legend. The Jewish Talmud. Muhammad's Alcheron.*

The *Legend, Talmud,* and the *Alcheron,*
Are differing lies, for one intention,
They work for differing works fram'd on one frame,
Like, lewd, large lies, fit for the whet-stone game:
One way they tend, though feveral ways proceed,
He well believes, who makes them not his Creed.

79. *To an Armenian Canary Bird.*

Thou that think'st good works in *God's* nose so savory,

What favour think'st thou smells he in thy
knavery?

80. *Faith without Works, Works without Faith.*

To believe and live ill, is but to think,
Without *Faith's* salt, *Good-works* will quickly stink.

81. *Ungirt, Unblessed.*

Ungirt, unblessed: a Proverb old, and good,
A true one too, if rightly understood:
unblessed he shall be everlastingly,
Who is not girt with *Christian verity.*

82. *True Charity.*

Not, who doth not, yet gladly would go to it,
Is Chaste, but he that may, and will not do it.

83. *From hardness of heart, good Lord deliver us.*

It's God alone that makes a tender heart.
To make hearts hard, ours and the Devil's part.

84. *A persuasion to Heaven.*

Where *Heaven* is, all our *Divines* agree,
They cannot well tell, where *Hell's* feet should be.
Why should we not, to known *Heaven* bend our
race?
Rather than by sin seek an unknown place?

85. *To a nameless Religious Friend.*

Why dost thou every *Sermon* God's Word call,
Since Preachers broach damn'd errors, flatter,
brawl?
Indeed thou maist *Sermons* this praise afford,
It is, or should be, *God's* own holy Word.

86. *To King* JAMES, *King of Great Britain, etc. of blessed memory.*

Our Ministers in their Evangeling,
Praying for thee; style thee *Great Brittain's King:*
Our Lawyers pleading in *Westminster* Hall,
Of *England,* and of *Scotland King* thee call.
For what great mystery, I cannot see,
Why Law, and Gospel should thus disagree.
Only I judge, that *Preachers* give thee thine,
By their Law its as lawful as Divine.

87. *The most Catholic King of Spain.*

The *Spanish King* is styl'd *Most Catholic:*
In it's hid a quaint mysterious trick,
His meaning is not in *Religion,*
But he intends it in *Dominion.*

88. *What use old Moons are put to.*

What doth become of old *Moons* thou dost ask,
And where her borrowed influence she shades?
For me to tell thee, t'were too hard a task,
A witty Wag says, They fill *Women's* heads.

89. *Little Legs, and less wit.*

At first me thought a wise man thou should'st be,
For *Calf* about thee I could no where see:
Tis thought thy *Calves* are walked into thy brain,
For all thy talk is in a *Calvish* vain.

90. *Problematically proving, that the City of Rome is not the seat of* CHRIST'S *Vicar General.*

Since *Christ* his old choice *City* ruined,
'Cause it despis'd *Him,* and his *Saints* blood shed,
Why should *He Rome,* with supreme *Grace* enable?
Who kill'd *him,* and of his innumerable?

91. *I prove it thus.*

Our Lord was Crucifi'd by *Pilat's* doom,
His death was Roman, and his *Judge* of *Rome,*
And of his death the chief pretended cause,
Was for the breach of *Rome's Imperial Laws:*
And the ten bloody persecutions,
Was by th'authority of *Rome's* great ones.

92. *Two Proverbs coupled.*

As those that get goods ill, do them ill spend,
So an ill life makes an ungodly end.

93. *Good Counsel, ill Example.*

Those that persuade others to *Godliness,*
And hue themselves ungodly ne'ertheless:
Are like a ships Cooke, that calls all to prayer,
And yet the greasy *Carle* will not come there.

94. *To an Upstart.*

Thine old friends thou forget'st, having got wealth:
No morale, for thou hast forgot thyself.

95. *Christ in the middest.*

He that on earth with low humility,
Betwixt two Thieves upon *Mount Calvary,*
Acted his Passive-active Passion,
In highest heaven in supreme dignity,
Seating himself betwixt the Deity,
Acts his Active-passive compassion.
O let me bear what thou dost act in me,
And act what may be suffered by *Thee!*

96. *God's Word is a two-edged Sword.*

God's Word wounds both ways like a two-edg'd Sword,
The *Preachers,* and the *Hearers* of the Word:

The fore edge wounds the *Hearers* on the pate,
The back-edge on the *Preachers* doth rebate.

97. *To the admirably witty, and excellently learned Sir* Nicholas Smith, *Knight, of Lorkbeare near Exeter, my ancient friend. Taking occasion of an Anigram of his. N.S.Tulaus mihi cos es.*

Praises on duller wits a sharp edge breeds,
Your Wit's all edge, he no such whet-stone needs.
Yet your steeled Judgement, sharp invention,
Tempered with learning, and discretion,
Millions of praises merits as their due:
Who knows you well, knows well that I speak true.

98. *To the right worshipful* William Noy, *Esquire, one of the Benchers of Lincoln's Inne, long since of my acquaintance both in Oxford and London.*

Noah the second father of all the souls,
Had in his *Ark* all beasts, and feathered fowls.
You in your *Ark,* as in a plenteous horde,
Have ster'd what *Wit,* or *Learning* can afford:
For all *Laws, Common, Ciuil,* or *Divine,*
For *Histories* of old, or of our time,
For *Moral Learning,* or *Philosophy,*
You are an exact, living *Library.*
But your rich mind mixed with no base allay,
Is ancient *Opher* of the old assay.
I may fear drowning, launch I further forth,
In the large, full, deep Deluge of your worth.

99. *To the right worshipful* Nicholas Ducke, *Esquire, one of the Benchers of Lincoln's Inn, and Recorder of the City of Exeter, my Cousin German.*

Although those Creatures, called by your name,
For their delight in dirt, deserve much blame,
And though that some of your profession,
Are glad when they have got possession.
Of the foul end, or will dirt a clear case:

You in your Circuittread a cleaner pase. I know it,
you abhor those sordid things,
and where 'twas foul before, you clear the
springs:
For which, wise honest men you high esteems,
May your young *Duckling* paddle in like streams.

100. *To the right worshipfull*Arthur Ducke, *Doctor of the Civil Law, and Chancellor of London, Bath and Wells, my Cousin German.*

To correct *Sin* and *Folly* to disgrace,
To find out *Truth,* and *Cunning* steps to trace,
To do this mildly, with an upright pace,
Are virtues in you fitted for your place.

101. *An Epithalamium. On the Marriage of Doctor* Arthur Ducke, *with one of the Daughters and Coheires of* Henry Southworth *Esquire.*

Amongst your best friends I am not ingrate
To *God,* who hath you given so good a mate,
Fair, Virtuous, Loving, with a great estate.
Would I had such another at the rate.

102. *To the right worshipful* William Hackwell *Esquire, one of the Benchers of Lincoln's Inne, my ancient kind friend.*

Your large, complete, solid, sufficiency,
Hid in the veil of your wise modesty,
Your quaint, neat learning, your acute quick wit,
And sincere heart, for great employments fit:
Beside your *Law,* wherein you do excel,
Because you little show of your great deal,
None can know well, except they know *you* well.

103. *To the Reverend* George Hackwell, *Doctor in Divinity, Archdeacon of Surry, my ancient & kind friend.*

Should I dilate all your great gifts at large,
Which for my weak *Muse* were too hard a charge,

An *Epigram* would to a volume grow,
If I their large particulars should show.
You have your brother's whole sufficiency:
Save for his *Law,* you have *Diuinity:*
This may I add, and with great joy relate:
For which to you oblig'd is our whole State,
In our blessed best plot, you have sow'd good seeds,
Which do out-grow *Natures* quick-growing weeds.

104. *To the right worshipful* John Barker *Esquire, late Mayor of the City of Bristol, my loving and kind brother in Law.*

Bristol your Birth-place (where you have augmented
Much, your much left you) is well recompensed.
In *Counsel Office,* and in *Parliament,*
For her good, you have show'd your good intent:
As you do grace the place, that did you breed,
I pray, your *Sons* sons may there so succeed.

105. *To the wise and learned S.B.K.Knight.*

A poet rich, a Judge, and a Just man,
In few but you, are all these found in one.

106. *To the right worshipful* John Doughty, *Alderman of Bristol, of his right worthy wife, my especial good friends.*

I have heard many say they'd not remarry,
If before them their kind wives should miscarry,
I fear, some of them from their words would vary.
Should your wife die, sad sole you would remain.
I have sufficient reason for my aim,
You cannot find so good a wife again.

107. *To the worshipful,* Richard Long *of Bristol, Merchant, and his good wife, my kind and loving friends.*

Unthankfulness is the great Sin of Sins,
But *Thankfulness* to Kindness, kindness wins.

For your dear love accept my thanks therefore.
An honest heart is griev'd he can no more.

108. *To the Reverend Doctor,* Thomas Winnife, *Dean of Glocester, Prebend of Paul's, and Chaplaine to King* CHARLES, *anciently of my acquaintance in Exeter College in Oxford.*

Your solid learning, and sincere behaviour,
Have worthily brought you into great favour,
And you are Deane of *Gloria Cesaris,*
Such *Chaplains* our great *Caesar's* glory is.

109. *To the right worshipful* Richard Spicer, *Doctor of Physicke, my loving and kind Kinsman.*

Apollo, first Inventor of your Art,
His hidden secrets doth to you impart,
Old *Galen, Auicen,* and all the rest,
Have with their knowledge your grave judgement blessed,
You are both wise and happy in your skill,
Doing continual good, and no man ill.

110. *To the right worshipful* Robert Vilvain, *Doctor of Physique, my ancient friend, in Exeter College in Oxford.*

Let me change your *Paternal* name *Vilvain,*
Somewhat more aptly, and call you *Feel-vain,*
In *Physique* still you are as good as any,
And with your *Recipe's* you have help't many,
Wherefore in troops the to sick you repair,
Who hath your help, need not of health despair.

111. *To the Reverend, learned, acute, and witty, Master* Charles Fitz-Geoffrey, *Bachelor in Divinity, my especial kind friend, most excellent Poet.*

Blind *Poet Homer* you do equalize,
Though he saw more with none, than most with eyes.
Our *Geoffrey Chaucer,* who wrote quaintly, neat,

In verse you match equal, him in conceit,
Featur'd you are like *Homer* in one eye,
Rightly surnam'd the Son of *Geoffrey.*

112. *To a right worshipful, discreet, sober Gentleman, a Justice of Peace, who of a wild demeaned young Gentleman, is now become a Reverend Minister, a painful Preacher, and a worthy Example.*

You know, I know, what kind of man you were;
Not like to make the man that now you are:
Your buds of *Grace,* were over-grown with folly,
These weeds plucked up, you are grown wholly holy,
From a strange, loose, wild waggish Libertine,
A *Doctor* learned, *Preacher* sweet, *Divine.*
Many take Orders, Livings to obtain.
Plenty you had, *Christ's* glory was your aim,
Your *Friends* joy'd much, when they saw you so given,
Ineffable's the joy that was in heaven.

113. *To the same Reverend Doctor.*

You are turn'd old Saint, leaving your young evils,
Whilst many young Saints, do become old Devils.

114. *To my honest Bed-fellow the privately Charitable, discreetly Beneficial, Master* Edward Payne, *Merchant of Bristol.*

Piein is *Greek,* to drink: *Pain, French,* for bread:
With *Pain* (God says) with these we shall be fed,
Yet without *Payne,* many these needfuls gain,
Only by thanking *God, and Master Payne.*

115. *To squint-eyed, envious* Momus.

For praising *These,* do not thou dispraise me;
If thou wilt be as these are, I'll praise thee.

116. *A little of my unworthy Self.*

Many of these were my familiars,
Much good, and goods hath fallen unto their shares,
They have gone fairly on in their affairs:
Good God, why have I not so much good lent!
It is thy will, I am obedient:
What thou hast, what thou wilt, I am content,
Only this breeds in me much heaviness,
My love to this Land I cannot express,
Lord grant me power unto my willingness.

117. *A Skeltonical continued rhyme, in praise of my New-found-Land.*

Although in clothes, company, buildings fair,
With *England, New-found-land* cannot compare:
Did some know what contentment I found there,
Always enough, most times somewhat to spare,
With little pains, less toil, and lesser care,
Exempt from taxings, ill news, Lawing, fear,
If clean, and warm, no matter what you wear,
Healthy, and wealthy, if men careful are,
With much-much more, than I will now declare,
(I say) if some wise men knew what this were,
(I do believe) they'd live no other where.

118. *A Napkin to wipe his mouth that waters at these deserved Commendations.*

Thus for this hopeful *Country* at this *Time*,
As it grows better, I'll have better *Rhyme.*

The Second Book of *Quodlibets*

1. *To the Reader of my reprehending general Epigrams.*

I Do not, nor I dare not *squib* the State:
Such *outrecuidant* sauciness I hate:
Nor do I mean any one *Man* herein;
In private terms, I lash a public sin;
If any guilty think I him do mean,
He judgeth right: for I at him do aim.

2. *Of the like Epigrams. To the right worshipful and learned,* Simon Baskervile, *Doctor of Physique.*

Epigrams are much like to *Oxymel,*
Honey and *Vinegar* compounded well:
Honey, and sweet in their invention,
Vinegar in their reprehension.
As sour, sweet *Oxymel,* doth purge though phlegm:
These are to purge *Vice,* take them as they mean.

3. *A problem of Children.*

Since God complains of too few Children,
And Satan hath for God's One, more than ten,
Yet still would have more. Why should *Man* alone
Repine at some, nay? wish that they had none?

4. *To a close Sinner, more fearful of shame, than Sin.*

David saith, *Stand in awe, and do not sin*
Thou standst *in awe,* but 'tis, lest thou be *seen.*

5. *To Curious Critic Wit, Head-Constable.*

Search close, thou maist some *Felony* find here:
From all Fool-hardy *Treason* these are clear.

6. *On* Erra Pater *and his Almanac.*

The often Printed *Gull-fool Erra Pater,*
Is in conclusion but an *erring prater.*

7. *To Baldpate.*

Surely, *Paldpate,* thou some times hadst a *brow*

Before thou lost thy hair; *No man* knows how.
Thy brow doth now reach home unto thy crown,
But uncrown'd thou art, he comes further down;
How far he comes, now cannot be descried:
For he comes down, down, down to thy *backside.*

8. *To a Paultry Acquaintance.*

Thou dost accuse me, and condemn my Rhymes,
Because to thee I dedicate no lines.
Thou dost as well deserve an *Epigram,*
As *Baldpate,* who is trim'd with many a one.

9. *To a certain Periwiggian.*

Thy smooth, sleek head-hair, daily settled on,
Though some say not, I saw it is thine own,
Thou paid'st for't: yet the hair thou hast lost,
When thou did'st lose it, did thee much more cost.

10. *Of the Antiquity of the true Church, to a Jesuit.*

Thou does demand, and acclamations raise,
Where our belief was, before *Luther's* days?
As *Christ* did answer to a question,
By such a like expostulation:
So do I ask, answer me when thou please,
Where was your *Faith,* long since the *Apostle's* days?

11. *To the same Jesuit.*

Art thou a *Jesuit,* yet dost us reproach
With want of *Faith,* ere *Luther* his did broach?
Your *race* was raiz'd, since he preach'd: your new errors
Are odious to your own, to others terrors.
A hated race, spew'd in these latter days,
Though Fathers cal'd, y'are the *Popes Roaring boys.*

12. *To a sober, sly, Penurious, Usurious Companion.*

Godliness is great gain, God says no less,
But thou saist, thou canst make gain godliness:
What thou hast got by *craft, and Usury,*
Thou wilt bequeath in *deeds of Charity.*
Such distribution I do emulate;
The way unto it, I abominate.

13. *The Indefatigability of a Shrew's Tongue.*

What long wants natural rest, cannot endure:
In all things, but a *Shrew's Tongue,* this is sure.

14. *The go-out and the Gout.*

Thou griev'd art with *the go-out, and the Gout;*
For if thy wife doth chide thee out of door:
Which of these ills is worst, some make a doubt:
I think *the go-out,* is the greater sore.
The *Gout* doth oft'nest but the great *Toe pain:*
The *go-out* doth afflict both *heart,* and *brain.*

15. *To Father* Taylor *Jesuit, sometimes my familiar friend in Oxford.*

You say that Images are *Laymen's Books.*
He learns most error, that most on them looks.
And to say truth, whatever you do say,
They're fit Books for the Learned, not the Lay.

16. *To an Idol worshipper, or an obstinate Recusant.*

Idols are senseless, speak them foul or fair;
And those that trust in them, as senseless are.
Trusting in them, thou art obdurate made,
That *Law* not *Gospel* can thee not persuade.

17. *A Meditation for such simple innocent people as I am.*

Since thou *All-wise* hast made me not so *wise,*
With subtle *Serpents* for to *subtlize;*
Accept my *plainness,* and my good *intent,*

That with thy *Dove* I may be *innocent;*
From *subtle tricks* guard my *simplicity.*
And make me simple in subtlety.

18. *The force of Repentance.*

Our sin enforceth God to raise his hand:
But our *Repentance* doth the stroke withstand.

19. *Most men want somewhat.*

Some honest well-bent minds their *strength* is slack;
Strong men have *strength,* some of them *wisdom* lack;
Wise men have *wit;* But some want *honesty;*
Some men are neither *honest, strong,* nor *witty.*

20. *Too much, too little, hurts.*

Light Corn bears ground that's not with dressing dight;
Without some learning, wit grows vain and light;
As too much dressing cause weeds, rank, and bad:
So too much *Learning* makes a quick wit mad.

21. *Greatness and Love move not in one Sphere.*

Greatness soars upward; *Love* is downward mov'd;
Hence 'tis that *Greatness Loves* not, nor is Lov'd.

22. *To an envied Favourite, right worthy of his preferment.*

Envious, and *bad,* 'gainst vir*tue, goodness* fight;
Would *Good,* and *wise,* did understand *you right.*

23. *To a cashiered Favourite; who hath deserved his disgrace.*

I grieve at thy disgrace, blush at thy shame,
But this draws tears; Thou hast deserv'd the same.

24. *How Little, how Great.*

The least of all the fixed *Stars,* they say,

Is sometimes bigger than the earth and *Sea.*
Poor little I that from earth have my birth,
Am but a clod, compared to the *Earth.*
How little now, how great shall I be then,
When I in *Heaven,* like to a *Star* shall shine?

25. *On Young weekly News-writers & old Chroniclers.*

Currantiers lie by Ubiquity;
But Chroniclers lie by Authority.
News-writers, Travellers are, *Historians* old:
Travellers and old men to lie may be bold.
Not then, Not there, cannot their lies un*fold.*

26. *Conscience.*

Whilst *conscious men* of smallest *sins* have ruth,
Bold *sinners* count great *Sins,* but tricks of youth.

27. *To a weak brained Good-fellow.*

Thy brain is weak, *strong drink* thou canst *not bear:*
Follow my Rule, *Strong drink* do thou *forbear.*

28. *The only Foundation Rock of Christs Church, To the Divines of Rome.*

Out of the *Creed,* wherein we both consent,
Peter, I prove is not the *Rock Christ* meant.
Do we believe *in God of all the maker?*
In that, the *Jew* with us is a partaker.
Do we believe, that *Christ was born and died,*
And that he was unjustly *Crucifi'd?*
The Turk believes so, and says he did stand,
Till theirs came mediating at God's right hand.
That he shall *Judge* all that believe in him,
Both *Jew* and *Turk, Forgiveness of all sin*
Believe; the *flesh's Resurrection,*
The blessed *Saint's holy Communion,*
And *life eternal* almost as we do,
And that their *Church* is *Catholic,* and true.

They do believe *the Spirit's influence,*
Though not like us, but in a larger sense.
But all within our *Creed,* which doth conduce,
To prove *Christ Jesus* is *the only sluice*
Of our *Saluation,* and *God's only Son;*
In that, we *Christians* do believe alone.
This is the Rock whereon *Christ's Church* is built.
Take away this, all our Faith's frame will tilt.
And this was *Peter's* wise confession:
Whence I deduce this firm conclusion;
Not *Peter* his *confession* the *Rock* is,
And *Christ* said not, *On Thee,* but, *Upon This.*

29. *An honest wrong'd Man's Meditations.*

Since for my Love, Friends me unkindly serve,
God will not use me, as I do deserve.

30. *The good effects of Corrections.*

Sea-water, though't be salt, salt meats makes fresh;
So doth correction our ill lives redress.

31. *Preacher's Fame, and Aim.*

Young *Preachers,* to *do well,* do take much *pain,*
That all may *do well,* is old *Preacher's aim.*

32. *To the Reader.*

This one fault *(Reader)* pardon, and endure,
If striving to be brief, I grow obscure.

33. *A Christian Meditation.*

I hope, and I do faithfully believe,
That God in love will me *Salvation* give:
I hope, and my assured firm faith is,
God will accept my *Love* to him and his.
I hope, by faith his *Love* will me afford
All this only, through Jesus Christ our Lord.

34. *A Mess of Mistakers.*

Lewd, loose, *large* lust, is love with Familists.
Papists chief *Hope* in their own works consists.
Some *Protestants* on barren *Faith* rely.
Atheists have no *Faith, Hope,* nor *Charity.*

35. *An Appendix to this Epigram.*

Love is the fruit; *Hope* the leaves; *Faith* the tree.
Who hath a perfect *Faith,* hath all these three.
Only by such a *Faith* men saved be.

36. *A Guilty Conscience.*

When God did call to *Adam,* Where art thou?
He meant not thereby, where, or in what place?
God knew in which bush he was well enough:
But, Where art, *Adam?* that is, in what case?

37. *To give the Church of Rome her due. To a Separatist.*

Though thou art loathe to put it in thy *Creed,*
The Church of *Rome* is a *true Church* indeed:
So is a Thief a true, truly a man,
Although he be not truly a true one.
How is it that Children there baptized,
By other Christians Christians are agnized?

38. *To Quick silver headed Innovators.*

Because of the uncertainty of *Wits,*
Our Law commands a certainty in *Writs:*
For as good cause is our Church Liturgy
Wisely reduced to a certainty.
If that were yielded to that some men seek,
We should have new *Church-Service* every week.

39. *Fair Good Wives.*

Clear-skinned, true colour'd Wives, with exact
features,
With wife, mild, chaste *Souls,* are the best of

Creatures.

40. *Fair Shrews.*

Clear-skinned, fair colour'd Wives, with exact features,
With shrewd, lew'd wild minds, are the worst of creatures.

41. *A Problem hereupon.*

If sin flesh be so ill with an ill mind,
What is a foul outside thus inward lin'd?
A Trestick to these three,
Disticks by way of Answer.

42. *To all constant Bachelors, especially to my Good Friend Mr.* Roger Michell.

Charybdis one, the other *Sylla* is,
And though the first an harbour be of bliss,
You *steer* the safest course, these *Rocks* to miss.

43. *To an honest old doting Man, such as I may be, if I live a little longer.*

A *Liar* should have a good memory;
For want of it thou utterest many a *Lie,*
Thou dost remember many things in great:
But the particulars thou dost forget.
Thou tell'st thy *Lies* without ill-*thought or pain;*
Th'are no malicious *Lies,* nor *Lies* for gain.

44. *A Crew of Cursing Companions. To the Bishop of* Rome.

With *Bell, Book, Candle,* each Ascension day,
Thou cursest us who for thee yearly pray.
But on good *Friday* the *Greek Patriarch,*
Doth ban thee, branding thee, with this lewd mark,
He styles thee, *Father of Corruption,*
Of Ancient *Fathers* the corrupting *One:*

They saw long since thy knavish forgery,
As we now see thy *Purging Knavery.*

45. *To the same man.*

He that doth dead *Saints Relics* Idolize,
Their living writings lewdly falsifies.

46. *Envy's Diet.*

Old wits have several ways 'dressed *Enuy's* food;
Each hath his sauce (if rightly understood)
Her own heart, her own flesh, A Toad, A Bone,
Which she devoureth sitting all alone:
Though these are fair, This dish doth me best please,
When I find her gnawing a wreath of Bays:
For her chief food, *Is well deserved praise.*

47. *To a handsome Whore.*

One told me, what a pretty face thou hast;
And it's great pity that thou art not *chaste.*
But I did tell him, that did tell it me,
That if thou were not *Fair,* thou *chaste* wouldst be.

48. *The mad life of a mad Sea-man of War.*

He lives, and thrives by death, and by decay,
He drinks, swears, curseth, sometimes he doth pray,
That he may meet somewhat to be his prey,
And spends the rest in sleep, at meat, at play.

49. *Of the Gunpowder Holiday, the 5. of November.*

The *Powder-Traitors, Guy Fawkes,* and his mates,
Who by a Hellish plot sought Saints estates,
Have in our Calendar unto their shame,
A joyful *Holy-day* called by their *Name.*

50. *On these black Saints.*

The first day of November is alway,
All-*Saints'* feast, and the fifth, all-*Deuils' day.*

51. *To a great Gamester.*

Saint *Paul* doth bid us *Pray continually,*
But thou would'st rather *Play continually.*

52. *Most men are mistaken. To Mr.* Robert Grimes.

Good, bad, rich, poor, the foolish, and the sage,
Do all cry out against the *present age,*
Ignorance made us think our young *Times* good;
Our elder days are better understood;
Besides, griefs past we easily forget;
Present displeasures make vs sad, or fret.

53. *The Tree of Sanctification.*

First grows the Tree, and then the *Leaves* do grow;
These two must spring before the *fruit* can show:
Faith is a firm *Tree, Hope,* like shaking *Leaves,*
From these two, *Charity* her *Fruits* receives.
Faith without *Hope,* and *Love,* is a dead *Tree,*
Hope without *Love,* and *Faith,* green cannot be.
Love without *Hope* and firm Faith is no more
Then handsome Fruit without, rotten at core.

54. *Real presence* }{ *Each contradict Praying to Saints* }{ *the other.*

If Christ be real, corporeal in the *bread,*
After the *Consecrating* words are said:
What need you go to Saints, since you may take
him
And use him as you please like them that bake
him?

55. *An Antidote for Drunkards.*

If that your heads would ache before you drink

As afterwards, you'd ne'er be drunk, I think.

56. *Women's Tyers.*

Women's head-laces and high towering wires,
Significantly, rightly are called tyres;
They tire them and their Maids in putting on,
Tire Tyremakers, with variation.
I think to pay for them, doth *tire* some men;
I hope they'll *tyre* the Devil that invents them.

57. *The Giant.*

I'm but a man, though I in length exceed.

The Dwarf.

Though I want length, a *Man* I am indeed.

The Giant to the Dwarf.

My *Sir* out-shot the mark, begetting me. Thy
Father shot too short, when he made thee.

The Dwarf to the Giant.

Although short shooting often lose the game, To
over-shoot the mark, is as much shame.

58. *To a nameless Friend, whose head is said to be full of Proclamations.*

To fill the head with *Proclamations,*
Is no disgrace, so they be well penn'd ones.

59. *The good of punishment.*

Plagues make proud, big, swollen hearts, fall low
again:
As *Caustics* bate proud *flesh,* though with much
pain.

60. *A Chyrurgion's good qualities. To my good friend Mr.* P.S. *Chyrurgion.*

A Surgeon should have, well to use his art,
Lady's hands, Eagle's eyes, a Lion's heart.
Not one of these good properties you lack,
But when you hide them in the white strong Sack.

61. *A Pill to purge Bribery.*

Those that do live here by *Corruption,*
Shall dye in the next generation.

62. *Papistical faith.*

What a strange doubtful blind no-Faith you hold,
Which cannot be *imagined, held, or told?*
What *Lay-men* know not, *Clerics* do think they know,
Says the Pope otherwise, It is not so.
The *Weather-Cock* of your *Religion*
Is in the Pope's shifting Opinion.

63. *Some poor comfort for these Multifidians.*

If this *Pope,* Millions draws with him to Hell,
The next wise *Pope* may reset all things well.

64. *Spiritual weapons to encounter with Satan. To my loving and good Aunt, Mistress* Elizabeth Spicer *of Exeter, mother to Doctor* Richard Spicer *Physician.*

These are strong Arms to buckle with the Devil,
Fasting, Faith, Prayer, bearing, forbearing evil:
If with these weapons God do vs assist,
Satan will ne'er stand to it, nor resist.

65. *Confidence ill used, and Confidence abused.*

Cursed is he that puts his confidence
In Man: *Only in man is* the right sense.
And that *Man* shall like punishment receive,
Who doth an honest *Confidence* deceive.

66. *A Caveat for buyers and sellers.*

In this world *silly buyers* must beware:
In the next world, *dear sellers of bad ware.*

67. *To Politic Bankrupt.*

Thou hast broke five times; thou wilt break once more:
What a brave *Tilter* thou wouldst make therefore!

68. *A mad answer of a Mad man.*

One asked a Mad-man, if a wife he had?
A wife (quoth he) I never was so mad.

69. *A lusty Widow, to one of her Suitors.*

To have me, thou tell'st me, on me thou'lt *dote.*
I tell thee, Who hath me, on me must do 't,
I may be cozen'd; but sure if I can,
I'll have no *doting,* but a *doing* man.

70. *To Mammonists, who put their trust in uncertain Riches.*

Some have too many goods: some would have none:
You have too many, though you have but one;
For yellow *Mammon* is your God alone.

71. *God and Mammon.*

Service to God, and Mammon none can do:
Yet we may serve God, and have *Mammon* too.

72. *There is no fooling with Edge-tools. To a Friend.*

Thou hast sped well in many a former plot,
Thou undertook'st a great one, fail'st in that,
Men must have Mittens on, to shoo a Cat.

73. *My Judgement on Men of Judgement. To a kind Friend.*

Thou talk'st of men of Judgement. Who are they?
Those, whose conceits success doth still obey.

Wise men's, wise counsel, is but their conceits;
If they speed ill, they are sad wise deceits.

74. *To all the shrewd Wives that are, or shall be planted in New-found-land.*

If mad-men, Drunkards, Children, or a Fool,
Wrong *sober, discreet men* with tongue or tool,
We say, Such things are to be borne withal.
We say so too, if Women fight, or brawl.

75. *Some prevention for some of these misdoers.*

Mad men are bound; Drunkards are laid to sleep:
Fools beaten are; Toys Children quiet keep:
I wish unruly *Shrews* were turned to *Sheep.*

76. *Masters Behaviour. To my good Friend Master* Thomas Milware, *of Harbor-Grace in Newfound- land.*

Stern, cruel usage may bad servants fetter:
Wise gentle usage, keeps good servants better.

77. *Too much Familiarity breeds contempt.*

Though some wise men this *Proverb* do apply,
For a defence of their austerity;
I think this way this *Proverb* might be meant,
Chiding too oft, brings *Chiding* in contempt.

79. *The four Elements in Newfound-land. To the Worshipful Captain* Iohn Mason, *who did wisely and worthily govern there divers years.*

The Air, in *Newfound-Land* is wholesome, good;
The Fire, as sweet as any made of wood;
The Waters, very rich, both salt and fresh;
The Earth more rich, you know it is no less.
Where all are good, *Fire, Water, Earth, and Air,*
What man made of these four would not live
there?

80. *To all those worthy Women, who have any desire to live in Newfound-Land, specially to the modest & discreet Gentle-woman Mistress* Mason, *wife to Captain* Mason, *who lived there divers years.*

Sweet Creatures, did you truly understand
The pleasant life you'd live in *Newfound-land;*
You would with *tears* desire to be brought thither:
I wish you, when you go, fair wind, fair weather:
For if you with the passage can dispense,
When you are there, I know you'll ne'er come thence.

81. *To a worthy Friend, who often objects the coldness of the Winter in Newfound-Land, and may serve for all those that have the like conceit.*

You say that you would live in *Newfound-land,*
Did not this one thing your conceit withstand;
You fear the *Winters* cold, sharp, piercing air.
The love it best, that have once wintered there.
Winter is there, short, wholesome, constant, clear,
Not thick, unwholesome, shuffling, as 'tis here.

82. *To the right worshipful* Iohn Slany, *Treasurer to the Newfound-land Company, and to all the rest of that Honourable Corporation.*

I know, that wise you are, and wise you were:
So was *he* who this Action did prefer:
Yet some wise men do argue otherwise,
And say *you* were not, or *you* are not wise:
They say, *you* were not wise to undertake it:
Or that *you* are not wise thus to forsake it.

83. *Of the same Honourable Company.*

Divers well-minded men, wise, rich, and able,

Did undertake a plot inestimable,
The hopeful'st, easiest, healthiest, just plantation,
That ere was undertaken by our *Nation.*
When they had wisely, worthily begun,
For a few errors that athwart did run,
(As every action first is full of errors)
They fell off flat, retir'd at the first terrors.
As it is lamentably *strange* to me:
In the next age *incredible* 'twill be.

84. *To the right Honourable Sir* George Calvert, *Knight, late Principal Secretary to King* JAMES, *Baron of Baltimore, and Lord of Avalon in Newfound-land.*

Your worth hath got you Honour in your days.
It is my honour, you my verses praise.
O let your Honour cheerfully go on;
End well your well begun *Plantation.*
This holy hopeful work you have half done,
For best of any, you have well begun.
If you give over what hath so well sped,
Your solid wisdom will be questioned.

86. *To the same Nobleman.*

Yours is a holy just *Plantation,*
And not a justling *supplantation.*

86. *To the right worthy, learned and wise, Master* William Vaughan, *chief Undertaker for the Plantation in Cambrioll, the Southernmost part of Newfound-Land, who with pen, purse, and Person hath, and will prove the worthiness of that enterprise.*

It joy'd my heart, when I did understand
That yourself would your *Colony* command;
It griev'd me much, when as I heard it told,
Sickness had layed on you an unkind hold.
Believe me, Sir, your *Colchos Cambrioll*
Is a sweet, pleasant, wholesome, gainful soul.
You shall find there what you do want; Sweet

health:
And what you do not want, as sweet; Sweet wealth.

87. *To the same industrious Gentleman, who in his golden golden-fleece styles himself* Orpheus Junior.

Your noble humour indefatigable,
More virtuous, constant yet, then profitable,
Striving to do good, you have lost your part,
Whil'st lesser loss hath broke some *Tradesman's* heart:
Yet you proceed with person, purse and pen,
Fitly attended with laborious men.
Go on, wise Sir, with your old, bold, brave *Nation*
To your new *Cambrioll's* rich *Plantation,*
Let *Dolphins* dance before you in the floods,
And play you, *Orpheus Junior,* in her woods.

88. *Some Diseases were never in* Newfound-land. *To the right worthy Mistress,* Anne Vaughan, *wife to Doctor* Vaughan, *who hath an honourable desire to live in that Land.*

Those that live here, how young, or old soever,
Were never vexed with Cough, nor Aguish Fever,
Nor ever was the Plague, nor small Pox here;
The *Air* is so salubrious, constant, clear:
Yet *scurvy Death* stalk here with thievish pace,
Knocks one down here, two in another place.

89. *To Sir* Richard Whitborne, *Knight, my dear friend, Sometime Lieutenant to Doctor* Vaughan *for his Plantation in* Newfound-Land, *who hath since published a worthy book of that most hopeful Country.*

Who preaching well, doth do, and live as well,
His doing makes his preaching to excel:
For your wise, well-penned Book this Land's your debtor;
Do as you write, you'll be believ'd the better.

90. *To my good Friend Mr.* Thomas Rowley, *who from the first Plantation hath liv'd in* Newfound-Land *little to his profit.*

When some demand, Why rich you do not grow?
I tell them, Your *kind nature* makes it so.
They say, that here you might have gotten wealth.
Adam in *Paradise* undid himself.

91. *There is more gain in an honest Enemy, than in a flattering Friend.*

A flattering Friend in's Commendations halts:
An honest Foe will tell me all my faults.

92. *To the right Honourable, Sir* Henry Cary, *Knight, Viscount* Faukeland, *Lord Deputy of* Ireland.

I joy'd when you took part of *Newfound-Land;*
I griev'd, to see it lie dead in your hand:
I joy'd when you sent people to that Coast;
I griev'd, when I saw all that great charge lost.
Yet let your *Honour* try it once again,
With wise, stayed, careful honest-hearted men,
I am to blame, you boldly to advise:
For all that know you, know you wondrous wise:
Yet near-hand, Dull blear-ey'd may better see,
Than quicker clear-ey'd, that a far off bee.

93. *To the Honourable Knight, Sir* Percivall Willoughbie, *who, to his great cost, and loss, adventur'd in this action of* Newfound-Land.

Wise men, wise Sir, do not the fire abhor,
For once being sing'd, more wary grow therefore.
Shall one disaster breed in you a terror?
With honest, meet, wise men mend your first
error.
If with such men you would begin again,
Honor and profit you would quickly gain.
Believe him, who with grief hath seen your share,
'Twould do you good, were such men planted

there.

94. *To my very good Friend, Mr.* John Poyntz, *Esquire, one of the Planters of* Newfound-Land *in Doctor* Vaughan's *Plantation.*

'Tis said, wise *Socrates* look't like an Ass;
Yet he with wondrous sapience filled was;
So though our *Newfound-Land* look wild, salvage,
She hath much wealth penn'd in her rusty Cage.
So have I seen a lean-cheeks, bare, and ragged,
Who of his private thousands could have bragged.
Indeed she now looks rude, untowardly;
She must be decked with neat husbandry.
So have I seen a plain swarth, sluttish *Jone,*
Look pretty pert, and neat with good clothes on.

95. *To the right Honourable Knight, Sir* William Alexander, *Principal, and prime Planter in* New-Scotland: *To whom the King hath given a Royal gift to defray his great charges in that worthy business.*

Great *Alexander* wept, and made sad moan,
Because there was but one *World* to be won.
It joys my heart, when such wise men as you,
Conquer new Worlds which that *Youth* never knew.
The King of Kings assist, bless you from Heaven;
For our King hath you wise assistance given.
Wisely our King did aide on you bestow:
Wise are all Kings who all their gifts give so.
'Tis well given, that is given to such a One,
For service done, or service to be done.
By all that know you, 'tis well understood,
You will dispense it for your Countries good.
Old *Scotland* you made happy by your birth,
New-Scotland you will make a happy earth.

96. *To the same Wise, Learned, Religious Patriot, most Excellent Poet.*

You are a *Poet*, better there's not any,
You have one super-virtue 'mongst your many;
I wish I were your equal in the one,
And in the other your Companion.
With one I'd give you your deserved due,
And with the other, serve and follow you.

97. *To the right Honourable, Sir* George Calvert, *Knight, Baron of* Baltimore, *and Lord of* Avalon *in* Britaniola, *who came over to see his Land there,* 1627.

Great *Shebae's* wise Queen travelled far to see,
Whether the truth did with report agree.
You by report persuaded, laid out much,
Then wisely came to see, if it were such:
You came, and saw, admir'd what you had seen,
With like success as the wise *Sheba* Queen.
If every *Sharer* here would take like pain,
This Land would soon be peopled to their gain.

98. *To the same right wise, and right worthy Noble- man.*

This shall be said whil'st that the world doth stand,
Your *Honor* 'twas first *honoured* this *Land.*

99. *To the right worshipful Planters of Bristol-Hope in the new Kingdom of Britaniola.*

When I to you your *Bristol-Hope* commend,
Reck'ning your gain, if you would thither send,
What you can spare: You little credit me:
The mischief is, you'll not come here and see.
Here you would quickly see more than myself:

Then would you style it, *Bristols-Hope* of wealth.

100. *To the right worshipful* William Robinson *of Tinwell, in Rutland shire Esquire, come over to see Newfound-Land with my Lord of Baltimore.* 1627.

Strange, not to see stones here above the ground,
Large untrenched bottoms under water drown'd.
Hills, and Plains full of trees, both small, and great,
And dryer bottoms deep of Turf, and Peat.
When *England* was us'd for a Fishing place,
By Coasters only, 'twas in the same case,
And so unlovely't had continued still:
Had not our *Ancestors* us'd pains, and skill:
How much bad ground with mattock and with spade,
Since we were born, hath there been good ground made?
You, and I rooted have Trees, Brakes, and stone:
Both for succeeding good, and for our own.

101. *To the first Planters of Newfound-land.*

What aim you at in your *Plantation?*
Sought you the *Honour* of our *Nation?*
Or did you hope to raise your own *renown?*
Or else to add a Kingdom to a *Crown?*
Or *Christ's* true *Doctrine* for to propagate?
Or draw Salvages to a blessed state?
Or our o're peopled *Kingdom* to relieve?
Or show *poor men where* they may *richly live?*
Or poor men's children godly to maintain?
Or amid *you at your own sweet private gain?*
All these you had *achiv'd* before this day,
And all these you have balk't by your delay.

102. *To my Reverend kind friend, Master* Erasmus Sturton, *Preacher of the Word of God, and Parson of Ferry Land in the Province of Avalon in Newfound-Land.*

No man should be more welcome to this place,
Than such as you, Angels of *Peace,* and *Grace;*
As you were sent here by the *Lord's* command,
Be you the blessed *Apostle* of this Land;

To Infidels do you Evangelize,
Making those that are *rude, sober* and *wise.*
I pray that *Lord* that did you hither send,
You may our *cursings, swearing, jovring mend.*

103. *To my very loving and discreet Friend, Master* Peter Miller *of Bristol.*

You asked me once, What here was our chief dish?
In Winter, Fowl, in Summer choice of Fish.
But we should need good Stomaches, you may think,
To eat such kind of things which with you stink,
As *Ravens, Crows, Coyotes, Otters, Foxes, Bears,*
Dogs, Cats, and Soils, Eagles, Hawks, Hounds, & Hares:
Yet we have *Partridges,* and store of *Deer,*
And that (I think) with you is pretty cheer.
Yet let me tell you, Sir, what I love best,
It's a *Poor-John* that's clean, and neatly dressed:
There's not a meat found in the Land, or Seas,
Can Stomachs better please, or less displease,
It is a fish of profit, and of pleasure,
I'll write more of it, when I have more leisure:
There and much more are here the ancient store:
Since we came hither, we have added more.

104. *To some discreet people, who think any body good enough for a Plantation.*

When you do see an *idle, lewd,* young man,
You say he's fit for our *Plantation.*
Knowing yourself to be *rich, sober, wise,*
You set your own worth at an higher price.
I say, such men as you are, were more fit,
And most convenient for first peopling it:
Such men as you would quickly profit here:
Lewd, lazy Lubbers, want wit, grace, and care.

105. *To the famous, wise and learned Sisters, the two Universities of England, Oxford and Cambridge.*

The ancient *Jews* did take a world of pain,
And travelled far some *Proselytes* to gain:
The busy pated *Jesuits* in our days,
To make some theirs, do compass Land and Seas:
The *Mohammedan, Heathen,* modern *Jew,*
Do daily strive to make some of their crew:
Yet to our shame we idly do stand still,
And suffer God, his number up to fill.
Ye worthy *Sisters,* raze this imputation,
Send forth your Sons unto our *New Plantation;*
Yet send such as are *Holy, wise,* and *able,*
That may build *Christ's Church,* as these do build
Babel.
If you exceed not these in *Righteousness,*
I need not tell your *Wisdoms* the success.

106. *To answer a Friend, who asked me, Why I did not compose some Encomiastics, in praise of Noble men and Great Courtiers, As my friend* John Owen *hath done.*

I knew the Court well in the old *Queen's* days;
I then knew *Worthies* worthy of great praise:
But now I am there such a stranger grown,
That none do know me there, there I know none.
Those few I here observe with commendation,
Are *Famous Stars* in our *New Constellation.*

The Third Book of *Quodlibets*

1. *Justice Epigram.*

Kings do correct those that *Rebellious* are,
And their good *Subjects* worthily prefer:
Just Epigrams reprove those that *offend,*
And those that *virtuous* are, *she* doth commend.

2. *To my delicate Readers.*

When I do read others neat, dainty lines,
I almost do despair of my rude rhymes:
Yet I have fetch't them far, they cost me dear,
Dear and far-fetched (they say) *is Ladies' cheer.*

3. *To my zealous, and honest friend, Master* W.B. *of Bristol.*

If thou canst not to thy preferment come,
To be *Christ's red Rose* in *best* martyrdom;
With *Patience, Faith, Hope, Love, and Constancy,*
A pure *blessed, white Rose* in *Christ's* Garden die.

4. *God's Love: The Devil's Malice.*

He that *made* man, only desires man's *heart:*
He that *marred* man, tempts man in every part.

5. *God rewards thankful men.*

What part of the *Moon's* body doth reflect
Her borrowed beams, yieldeth a fair prospect;
But that part of her, that doth not do so,
Spotty, or dark, or not at all doth show:

So what we do reflect on *God the giver,*
With thankfulness: those *Graces* shine for ever:
But if his *gifts* thou challeng'st to be thine,
They'll never do the *Grace,* nor make thee shine.

6. *To a dissembling, sober, sly Protester.*

'Tis so, or so, *as I'm an honest man,*
Is thy assuring *Protestation,*
When it's *as true* as thou art *such a one.*

7. *Dissemblers cozen themselves.*

Whilst in this life *Dissemblers* cozen some,
Themselves they cozen of the life to come.

8. *On a wide-mouthed prating companion.*

He prates, and talks, and rails and no man hears.
Yet he hath *mouth,* to make a score of Ears.

9. *Latin Prayers by number.*

Christ spake no *Latin,* though he could do so,
Nor any of his *Twelve,* for ought I know.
Why should you in that tongue pray by the score?

It is the *Language* of the *Mounted Whore.*
Somewhat more merrily; here lies the jest:
Most of *hers* speak the *Language* of *her Beast.*
In such *Hobgoblin* words they sing, and pray,
Scaliger full-tongued knows not what they say.

10. *To the Bishop of* Rome.

Of Bishops I dare stile *you Principal,*
'Tis *Anti-Christian* to be *General.*

11. *A wife more dear than sweet. To a complementing kind Husband.*

Come hither, *dear wife,* prithee *sweet wife* go,
Sweet wife, do this, or *dear wife,* pray' do so.
She's *dear* indeed, but not so *sweet,* I trow.

12. *Plasters for a Gald-heart.*

On every married man that hath a *Shrow,*
(As many a married man hath one, I trow;)
These sour, poor, piteous *plasters* I bestow,
Except their wives death, the best help I know.
1. Or to thy friend reveal thy woeful plight;
2. Or let her hot words thee inflame to fight;
3. Or else withdraw thyself from her by flight;

4. Or with thy patience all her wrongings slight.

13. *A husband's desire to his Wife.*

Laugh with me, make me *laugh,* whilst I do live:
When I die, choose where thou'lt *laugh* or grieve.

14. *To a weeping Widow.*

Thy *Husband's* dead, and thou dost *weep* therefore,
No: 'tis, cause thou canst make him *weep* no more.

15. *Ill-favoured Housewifery. To one shrewdly married.*

Though you fall out, yet you agree herein,
When as thy wife doth wash, then do'st thou wring.

16. *To all Choleric People.*

Shrewdness is like unto a *Gravesend toast,*
Abhorred by those that do use it most.
In us we do contentedly it bear,
We cry, Fought at it, finding it else-where.
If *Shrews* say they cannot their Choler smother,
I say, For health's sake we must vent that other.
'Tis hugg'd *at home, abroad,* at home it is abhor'd,
Thence I conclude *Shrewdness* is like a T.

17. *To those who I fear will find fault with this Comparison.*

If you will say that this is odious,
Comparisons are so; this should be thus.

18. *Reasons for the taking of Tobacco.*

Since most *Physicians* drink *Tobacco* still,
And they of nature have th'exactest skill,
Why should I think it for my body ill?
And since most *Preachers* of our *Nation,*
Tobacco drink with moderation,
Why should I fear of prophanation?
Yet if that I take it intemperately,
My soul and body may be hurt thereby.

19. *The fine Properties of good Tobacco.*

Tobacco to be good, it must be *strong,*
Clear smok't, white ashes, hard and *lasting long.*

20. *A City Sheriff.*

Before, and after, sparing he doth live,
Bravely he spends, when he is *Master Shrieve.*

21. *Si Senior: Spaniard. Signore Si: Italian.*

Of *Spaniards* and *Italians* thus I find,
As Arse-verse *they* aver their mind.
So one before, the other fins behind.

22. *Why* Astrea *left the Earth.*

On earth *Astrea* held the Balance even:
But she long since with them is fled to heaven,
Why hath *Astrea* bid this world Adieu?
Her Leaf was out, She would not buy a new.

23. *On a Private, Rich, close-liuing Churl, alluding to him in* Terence, *who of himself says, Populus me fibulat, &c.*

Walking abroad like a great *Turkey-Cock,*
Some steer, some jeer, ev'ry one doth me mock:
At home amongst my *puddings* and my *eggs,*
I hug myself, looking on my full bags,
Finding myself Fortune's white soon to be,
I laugh at them, that even now laugh't at me.

24. *To the same fellow.*

Thou art deceiv'd, self-flattering-golden *Ass,*
Whil'st thou behold'st thyself in a false *Glass.*

25. *To the Pope.*

Christ said unto the people, *Reade and see*
The Scriptures: for *they testify of me.*
Wherefore didst thou thine reading them deny?
That thou art *Antichrist,* they testify;

26. *Papistical cruelty.*

Were there no other argument but this,
It proves our faith, then yours the better is.
We are not cruel, bloody, envious,
(Though your late-lying *Legends* slander us)
We meekly seek but your *Conversion,*
Weep at your sought for *Execution:*
You bloody, slanderous, and inexorable
At all times, everywhere, where you are able:
Witness *Mary's* short Reign, *French Massacre,*
Which in red letters, your lewd minds declare.
Our *God,* thou *Just,* his mercy's over all,
A blood-sucker, *Satan* was from his fall.

27. *A Prayer hereupon, to the God of Justice.*

When thou for blood mak'st inquisition,
Think on the bloody *Inquisition.*

28. *To our wise Roman Divines.*

Why enforce ye a *blind obedience?*
All else would see your *Glosses enforc't since.*

29. *Why the five-footed Iambic fits best in our English verse.*

Iambics in our language have best grace:
They with grave *Spondees* dance a Cinquepace:
If wanton *Dactyls* do skip in by chance,
They well-near mar the measure of the *Dance:*
To end a verse, she may a foot be lending,
Like to a round trick at a *Galliard's* ending.

30. *To the Divine soul of that excellent Epigrammatist, Master* John Owen.

Let thy *Celestial Manes* pardon me,
If like thy shadow I have followed thee.

32. *Why Preachers stand, and Auditors sit. To his loving Friend, Master Robert Burton.*

Would'st know why *Preachers stand,* and we do *sit?*
Because what they speak with, or without wit,
Not we, but they themselves must *stand* to it.

33. *What Prosperity cannot persuade, Adversity will enforce.*

He that in *Zeal* is calm, in calms at Sea,
In storms if he have *Zeal,* in *Zeal,* he'll pray;
So though our *Zeal* be cold whil'st *Fortune* shines,
'Twill be more fervent in tempestuous times.

34. *To a Friend.*

Show such as mine to young-brisk *Butterflies,*
(Who have as many hearts as they have eyes,)
They'll swear to you, *The best that e'er they saw:*
Behind your back, *They are not worth a straw.*
This shuffling shows, that in their Pussy-paste wit,
Momus and *Gnato* do at random fit.

35. *Talking Beasts.*

When *Aesop* said Beasts spake; *Aesop* said true.
I heard *Beasts* speak within this day or two.

36. *The Gout.*

'Tis said, that rich men only have the *Gout,*
Of that old-rusty-sad saw, I make doubt.
Indeed the *Gout,* the child is of *rich men;*
This froward Else, poor men *nurse* now and then.

37. *When I was at Lincoln's Inn, the fashion was, (and I think is still) after dinner upon grand and festival days, some young Gentlemen of the house would take the best Guest by the hand, and he the next, and so hand in hand they did solemnly pass about the fire, the whole Company, each after other in order; to every staff a song, (which I could never sing) the whole Company did with a join'd voice sing this burden:*
Some mirth and solace now let us make, To cheer our hearts, and sorrows stake. Upon this kind of Commencement of these Revels, I conceited this:

When wise, rich *Lawyers* dance about the fire,
Making grave needless mirth sorrows to slack.
If *Clients* (who do *them* too dearly hire,
Who want their money, and their comfort lack)
Should for their solace, dance about the Hall:
I judge their dance were more methodical.

38. *An old Proverb, though a strange one, truly exemplified.*

A Proverb 'tis, how true I cannot tell,
Happy are those, whose fathers go to hell,
Sure, some would think, their happiness it were,
If their close-fisted *fathers* in *hell* were,
That they may of his wealth have out their share.
For whil'st they live, but little they will spare.

39. *To a nameless one.*

Thou marri'st one, whom thou before didst know:
It is the fashion now to marry so.

40. *The first Arithmetic.*

Adam at first in *number* was but one;
Until *God added Eve,* he was alone:

They were *divided*, till the *Lord* them joins,
And bade them *multiply* out of *their Loins:*
And so from them *subtracted* are all *Nations,*
Unto these present *Generations.*

41. *The seeming good works of Unbelievers.*

The glorious deeds of *unbelieving* ones,
Are glittering clear *abominations;*
So said St. *Hurom:* and thus saith St. *Paul,*
They're shining brass, and a tinkling Cymbal.
For *good works* without *faith* and *loving fear,*
Do neither please *God's eye,* nor yet his ear.

42. *Heavenly, and Earthly hearts.*

The *Earth* is firm, the *Heavens* mutable,
Yet *Heavenly* minds are firm, *Earthly* unstable.

43. *To a superstitious Papist, fearful of Purgatory, who to his cost desires to have a quick dispatch from that fearful place.*

With *faith* pray fervently, *religious live;*
Thou need'st no money, for an *Obit leave,*
Thy soul in *Purgatory* to relieve.

44. *To rich Papists.*

If the *Popes Saves* by his *authority,*
Were truer than Christ's written *Verity;*
Those rich men, Asses were, that went to Hell,
If they within *Rome's Churches* limits dwell:
For though you ne'er so lewdly spend your breath,
Your Coin will buy you *Pardons* after death.

45. *An humble, contrite, and double-diuided heart.*

God's favour breaks forth on *a broken heart:*
But in *a parted one God* hath *no part.*

46. *A short Dialogue betwixt two ancient Philosophers, laughing* Democritus, *and weeping* Heraclitus.

Heraclitus.
Vain, foolish man, why dost thou always laugh?
Democritus.
Man's vanity, and foolish pride I scoff,
Wherefore dost thou such a strange puling keep?
Heraclitus.
For man's bad sins, sad miseries I weep.

47. *Counsel to my young Cousins,* John *and* William Barker, }{ *Sons to my Brother* Abel *and* Mathew Rogers, }{ Barker, *and his now wife.*

Ill Company is like Infection,
It soon taints a good disposition.
Take heed into what Company ye fall:
Vice is a sickness *Epidemical.*

48. *To one, who on his Gossips prattlings in a dangerous disease, thinks and hopes so much of his Recovery, that he neglects the consideration of his Mortality.*

'Cause some have seep'd that have been almost dead,
Thou think'st that thou may'st be recovered:
But because many healthy men do die,
I think on that, knowing that so may I.

49. *To my Reverend sick friend,* W.G. *of* Bristol.

When folk are sick, we say, *They are not well.*
My Country phrase is, *That they are not quiet.*
Both of these phrases fit all those that mell
With *Physic Doses,* and *prescribed diet.*
The first of these two phrases fit *sick men:*
The last fits best *Women* and *Children.*

50. *Papistical Miracles.*

Primitive miracles were strange and true,
And did confirm the *Doctrine* then held new.
Yours falsely, feign'd, ridiculous, and bold,

Bolster new Doctrines, contradict the old.
Your apparitions, new-feign'd miracles,
Do overthrow the *ancient Articles.*

51. *An Advertisement to all Tradesmen, and may serve for Soldiers, or any others subject to Casualty.*

Who doth refuse a reasonable *proffer,*
Had need to have good *Fortune* in his Coffer.

52. *To a Card-Cheater.*

To *Cut,* and *Shuffle,* in a Horse is ill:
To *shuffle,* and to *Cut,* is thy prime skill.

53. *To one that hath lost both his ears.*

Some that have *two ears,* hear not what we say:
Thou that hast *not an ear,* hear'st more than they.

54. *Whom Discretion doth not, Correction will keep under.*

If head-strong Jades will not *God's Bit* obey,
His *Rod* will whip their restiness away.
No quid nimis.

55. *A meditation of too much and too little Wind at Sea, wracking Storms, and starving Calms.*

Man's state on shore, is like man's state at Sea;
Too much, too little, causeth sad decay;
Hence Poets fained *Fortune* heretofore
Sailing, one foot on Sea, and one of shore.

56. *Fearful Hell-Fire.*

At sight of *fire,* bold Lions run away
Bold sinners, who men fearing sin, upbray:
The sight of *Hell-fire* will these Lads dismay.

57. *To Sir* Senix Fornicator.

Winter hath seiz'd upon thy beard, and head,
Yet for all this, thy wild Oates are not shed.

Me thinks when Hills are overspread with Snow,
It should not wantonly be hot below.
But thou most like unto a *Lecke* doth seem:
For though thy head by *white,* thy tail is *green.*

58. *Some standers by see more }{ then Gamsters.*
Some standers by lees more }{ then Gamsters.

Some wise by-standers more than Gamesters sees;
Some standers by more than wise Gamesters' lees.

59. *To nobly descended Recusants.*

'Tis said, you came from noble *Ancestors,*
Who did strange wonders in the old French wars,
You say you are of their Religion,
And that it is the *true and ancient one:*
It was your *Ancestors,* for ought I know:
But *new, untrue,* God's *old true* Word says so.

60. *Traditions and God's Word. To Papists.*

'Twixt your *belief,* and our *Religion,*
There hath been long, and strong contention:
You prove yours by *men's word:* but we abhor it:
Our proof is better, we have *God's Word* for it.

61. *To one that asks me why I do write so briefly.*

What I do write of, I but only touch,
Who writes of many things cannot write much, *Or thus,*
Who writes of many things, must needs write much.

62. *To my kind loving bedfellow, Mr.* Edward Payne, *on the Gift of a Ring, wherein there was a Poesie of Patience.*

In your last gift you wish me *Patience.*
I know you mean it in the better sense;

Not a sad, bad, stout *patience, Stoical.*
But one that knows, that God sends, and mends all.

63. *Wise men's ill success, and Fool's Fortune. A Paradox.*

As many *Wise men* hurt themselves through wit,
As there are *softs* grow rich, for want of it.

64. *To the Pope.*

Wherefore should'st thou blinds Ignorance enhance?
(On which all Wiser times did look askance?)
Saying it doth devotion much advance?
All thy mysterious skill, is Ignorance.

65. *One of the Pope's titles is, Servant of Servants.*

Servant of Servants, *Popes* themselves have nam'd,
By that stile cursed *Canaan* was defam'd.

66. *All things are vendible at* Rome.

In *Rome's* full shop *are sold* all kinds of *ware,*
Men's souls purg'd, fire-new, you may *buy* there.

67. *To fault-finding more faulty Zoilus.*

When others' faults thou dost with spite reveal,
The *Kettle twits the pot with his burnt tail.*

68. *To a hard-favour'd Widow, who, because she hath many Suitors, thinks well of herself.*

We know thee *rich,* and thou think'st thyself *fine:*
Thou think'st we love *thee,* we know we love *thine.*

69. *Why Physicians thrive not in* Bristol.

In *Bristol* Water-tumblers get small wealth:
There *Doctor good-wine* keeps them all in health.

70. *To my Readers. An Arse-verse Request, to my Friend* John Owen.

Do not with my leaves make thy backside bright:
Rather with them do thou *Tobacco* light.
I'd rather have them up in flames to fly,
Than to be stifled basely privily.

71. *Health and Wealth.*

Health is a Jewel, yet though shining *wealth,*
Can buy rich *Jewels,* it cannot buy *health.*

72. *To Invocators of Saints.*

To *Saints* you offer supplication,
And say, *God's* face beholding, they them know.
This is a strange bold *speculation.*
Whence came the *Doctor* that first told you so?
In *God's* Word we do read, that *God* sees all:
Of such a glass no mention made at all.

73. *To those Papists, who show their ignorant Devotion in their Ave Marias.*

How long shall Ignorance lead you astray?
Whil'st to our Lady you'd a prayer say,
You her salute, and needless for her pray.

74. *To one of the Elders of the sanctified Parlour of Amsterdam.*

Though thou maist call my merriments, my folly,
They are my Pills to purge my melancholy,
They would purge thine too, wert not thou *Fool-holy.*

75. *Great men's entertainment.*

Though *rich* men's *troubles, kinds* are esteem'd,
Yet *poor* men's *kindness, troubles* are still deem'd.

77. *To a Bad-minded, Choleric, ungrateful man.*

Thou soon forget'st those wrongs thou dost to Men:
All small wrongs done to thee thou dost

remember;
Every good turn thou dost, thou count'st it ten:
For good done to thee, thy record is slender.
Kindness from thee, like vomits make thee sweat;
Thou swallow'st others kindness as thy meat.

78. *To Master* Fabian Sanford, *Master of our Ship and voyage in Newfound-Land, and may serve for all Masters trading there.*

Men wearied are with *labour* other-where:
But you are weary, when you want it here.
And what in *England* would quite tire a horse,
Here the want of it, tires you ten times worse.
Labour was first a curse to curb man's pride;
The want of it, makes you to *curve, chafe, chide.*
To see you work thus, better would me please,
Did you not work thus upon *Sabbath Days.*

79. *Goodness and Greatness. To my good and loving Cousin, Mistress* Thomasin Spicer, *wife to Doctor* Richard Spicer, *Physician.*

Goodness and *Greatness* falling at debate,
Which should be highest in men's estimate;
After much strife, they upon this did rest,
Great-goodness and *Good-greatness* is the best.

80. Mary Magdalene's *Tears. To my pretty Niece,* Marie Barker.

To wash *Christ's* feet, *Mary's Bath* was her *tears,*
To wipe them dry, her *Towel* was her *hairs:*
What her *tears* could not cleanse, nor *hairs makes dry,*
Her *Coral lips* did wipe, and mundify.
She did anoint him with a sweet, rich *oil,*
And spared for no cost, nor for no toil:
This Story merits to be Registered,
And to be practised as well as read.

81. *To my Niece and God-daughter,* Grace Barker.

I promised, you should do good, and fly ill,
Before that you had *power,* or *will,* or skill.
Lame Nature I knew could not walk that pace,
Without *God's Grace:* therefore I nam'd you *Grace.*
Let mild *Grace* so sway *Nature* in you then,
That you may obtain *Grace* with *God* and *Men.*

82. *To a nameless, wise, modest, fair Gentlewoman, my loving and kind Friend, whom reciprocally I love as heartily.*

Juno is wealth, *Pallas* is virtue, wit,
Venus Love, beauty is in *Poets'* writ:
Pallas, and *Venus* have in you their *treasure,*
Why should hard *Juno* offer us such measure?

83. *To our most Royal Queen* MARY, *Wife, Daughter, and Sister to three Famous Kings.*

Venus, and *Pallas,* at your birth conspir'd,
To make a work, of all to be *admir'd:*
Venus with *admir'd* feature did you grace,
Divine complexion, an Angel-like face.
Pallas inspir'd a quick, sweet, nimble spirit,
Virtue, and wit, of *admirable* merit,
But I *admire* them most, how they could place
So much; so *admirable* in so small space:
And they themselves *admir'd* when they had ended,
A Piece which they knew could not be amended.

84. *To the same most Royal Queen.*

When wise *Columbus* offered his *New-land,*
To *Wise men,* they him held, vain, foolish, fond,
Yet a *wise Woman,* of an happy wit,
With god success aduentur'd upon it:
Then the wise-men their *wisdoms* did repent,
And their *heirs* since their follies do lament.
My *New-land (Madam)* is already known,
The way the air, the earth, all therein grown,

It only wants a *Woman* of your spirit,
To mak't a Land fit for your *Heirs* t'inherit.
Sweet, dreaded *Queen,* your help here will do well:
Be here a *Famous second Isabel.*

85. *A Newfound-land Poetical Picture, of the admirable exactly featur'd young Gentlewoman, Mistress* Anne Lowe, *eldest Daughter to Sir* Gabriel Lowe, *Knight, my delicate Mistress. The Preface to her Picture.*

At sight, Love drew your picture on my heart,
In *Newfound-Land* I limm'd it by my Art.

86. *The Portrait.*

If *Paris* upon *Ida* hill had seen
You 'mongst the *Three,* the *Apple* yours had been.
Had curious *Zeuxis* seen your-all-excelling,
Whilst *Juno's* Picture he was pencilling;
You had him eas'd in his *various collection:*
For *Beauty* hath in you a full *Connection.*

87. *To the fair and virtuous Gentlewoman, Mistress* Mary Winter, *the younger, worthy of all love.*

Your budding beauty, wit, grace, modesty,
I did admire, even in your infancy,
These blessed buds, each grown to a fair flower,
Much have I lov'd, since my first lawful hour.
Whom few *cross-Winters* have made old and sad,
One such fair *Winter* would make young and glad.

88. *To the same beauteous modest Virgin,* an Enigma.

Had not false shuffling *Fortune* paltered,
Hymen had *Hyems* long since altered.

89. *To a fair modest Creature, who deserves a worthy name, though she desires here to be nameless.*

Niggardly *Venus* beauty doth impart
To divers diversely, and but in part.

To one a dainty Eye, a cherry Cheek:
To some, a tempting Lip, Breasts white and sleek:
To divers' ill-shap'd bodies, a sweet face:
Clean made Legs, or a white hand, doth some grace,
On *Thee* more free her gifts *She* doth bestow;
For *She* hath set *Thee* out in *Folio.*

90. *To my outwardly fair, and inwardly virtuous kind friend, Mistress* Marie Rogers, *widow, since married to Master* John Barker *of Bristol, Merchant, my kind and loving Brother in Law.*

Lilies, and *Roses* on your face are spread,
Yet trust not too much to your *white* and *red:*
Lilies will fade, Roses their leaves will shed:
These flowers may die, long before you are dead.
Your *inward beauty* (which all do not see)
Then *white and red,* and *you,* more lasting be.

91. *To the fair, virtuous, witty widow, Mistress* Sara Smeyths.

If it be true, (as some do know too well;)
To *Lovers' Heaven,* we pass through *Lovers' Hell:*
Be confident, you shall enjoy *Earths glory,*
For you on *Earth* are past your *Purgatory.*

92. *To my kind and worthy Friend, Mistress E.B. wife to Captain H.B. By my Captain's leave.*

Your *outward,* and your *inward graces* move
My *tongue* to *praise* you, and my *heart* to *love.*
I hope, it will not *God,* nor *man* offend,
If that in *Love* your *virtues* I *commend:*
And by his *Leave* who is yours in possession,
I'll *love,* and *praise* your goodness in reversion.

93. *To my perpetual Valentine, worthy Mistress* Mary Tayler, *wife to Master* John Tayler *Merchant of Bristol.*

My sweet discreet perpetual Valentine,
In your fair breast *virtue* hath built a *Shrine,*

Bedecking it with flowers, *amongst* the rest,
Mild bearing *your not-bearing* is not least.
You know the worthy *husband* that you have,
Is worth more *children* than some fondlings crave;
Besides the blessed *babes* begot by good,
More comforts bring than some of flesh and blood.
Kind *Valentine,* still let our comfort be,
Children there are enough for *you* and *me.*

94. *To my best Cousin, Mistress Elizabeth* Flea, *wife to Master* Thomas Flea, *of Exeter Merchant.*

If one were safely lodg'd at his long rest,
I could with you a *Flea* in my warm nest.
Who writes this, loves *Ye* both so well, he prays,
Long may ye skip from *Death,* like nimble *Fleas.*

95. *To the fair modest Maid, pretty Mrs.* Martha Morris, *and of her handsome sister, Mistress* Marie Philips, *both of Bristol.*

Though *Martha* were with *Mary* angry for't,
Yet *Christ* told her, *She* chose the better part.
Faire, chaste maid *Martha,* you have chose the best:
Your sister *Mary,* a life of less rest.

96. *Another to the same, being since married.*

But since I hear that you have chang'd your state,
I wish your choice may prove kind, fortunate,
And that he may deserve you every deal;
He well deserves, that doth deserve you well.

97. *To the pretty, pert, forward green, Mistress L.B.*

Nature took time your pretty parts to form,
She hastes her work in you, since you were born,
Your *buds* are forward, though your *leaves* are green:
I think you will be ripe at Eleventeen.

98. *To the modest, and virtuous Widow, Mistress* Eli- zabeth Gye *of Bristol, whose dead Husband Master* Philip Gye, *was sometimes Governour of the Plantation in* Newfound-Land, *where he, and she lived many years happily and contentedly.*

Though Fortune press you with too hard a hand,
I hear, your heart is here, in *Newfound-Land.*

99. *To a debauched University. A Complaint against Drunkenness.*

Thy Sons *(most famous Mother)* in old time,
To quench their thirst, *Pernassus* hill did climb.
Some of thy Sons, now think that hill too steep,
Their *Helliconian* springs do lie more deep.
Their study now is, where there is good drink,
The *Spigot* is their *Pen,* strong beer their *Ink.*
I could with *Democrit'* laugh at this sin,
If it in any other place had bin:
But in a place where all should be decent,
A sin so nasty, inconvenient,
So beastly, so absurd, worthy disdain,
It strains me quite out of my merry strain.
I could with *Heraclit'* lament, and cry,
Or write complaints with woeful *Jeremy:*
Nay, much-much more, if that would expiate

What's past, or following follies extirpate.
Many *rare wits* hath it infatuate,
Their climbing merits quite precipitate,
And hopes of ancient houses ruined.
Fools and base *sots* this sin hath made of them,
That by sobriety had been brave men:
Yea I do know, many wise men there be,
Which for this dare not trust their Sons with thee,
Fearing this *Cerberus,* this *Dog of Hell,*
Within whose Ward all other follies dwell.
I hope, thy Sister better looks to hers,
Indulgent *Elies* are thy Officers,

If they will not assist my motion,
To apply *Caustics,* and no *Lotion;*
Dear Mother, on my knees I beg this boon,
Afford this inconvenient Vice no room,
But whip it in thy *Convocation,*
Or strip it of *Matriculation.*

100. *A short Jig after this long Lachryvsa Pauin.*

As drunk as an old Beggar, once 'twas said.
As drunk as a young Scholar, now we read.

101. *To the Reverend, Learned, Sober, and wise Governors in this Famous University.*

I hear, this sin you will shut out of door:
It joys me so, that I can write no more.

102. *That every one may take his. To my worthy Readers.*

Fair, modest, learned, sober, wise, and witty,
Praising I praise you, if those praises fit ye.

103. *To my unworthy Reader.*

Fond, wicked, misled, if thou guilty be,
Although I name thee not, yet I mean thee.

The Fourth Book of *Quodlibets.*

An Unfinished Book.

1. *To the Reader.*

Sermons and Epigrams have a like end,
To improve, to reprove, and to amend:
Some pass without this use, 'cause they are witty;
And so do many Sermons, more's the pity.

2. *To the Reader.*

Of my small course, poor *wares* I cannot boast:
Owen and others have the choice engrossed:
And if that I on trust have ta'ne up any;
Owen hath done so too, and so have many.

3. *Redargution or paid with his own money.*

When *Pontius* call'd his neighbour, Cuckold Ass,
Being mad to see him blinded, as he was,
His Wife him standing by, repli'd anon:
Fie, *Husband,* fie, y'are such *another man.*
Nay, I do know (quoth *Pontius*) that there be
Nine more in Town, in as bad case as he.
Then you know ten, if you (quoth she) say true.
Fie, *Husband,* fie, what an *odd man* are you?

4. *Catholic, Apostolic Roman faith. To Papists.*

If the word *Catholic* ye truly strain,
To neither of us doth it appertain.
Apostolic we dare ourselves afford,
And prove it by their practice, and their word.
The now new Roman Faith ye stiffly hold,
And brag of it, as if it were the old.

5. *To elder Pelagians, more fine later Papists and our refined Arminians.*

Though sev'ral ways you one opinion twine,
'Twixt your conceits there's but a little line:
For all of you with *free-grace* are too bold,
With good works laying on presumptuous hold.
With your weak works, binding your boundless

Maker,
Without whom, none can be an undertaker.
Whilst *God* ties us by Faith to do good *deeds,*
You will *tie God* to you by your fond *Creeds.*
Satan, that lowers at *faithful, fearful* works,
Likes your *good deed,* because he knows your quirks.
At weak, faith-propped, due works Satan doth grieve:
At tip-toe good works, he *laughs* in his sleeve.
It's *God* that gives us grace, and makes us able,
Having all done, we are unprofitable.
Work, and work on with fond credulity,
Mercy with *faith* is our security.

6. A Chronogram *of the year wherein Queen* Elizabeth *died, and King* James *came to the Crown of* England: *both of blessed memory. We Made a Happy Change this Year. MDCIII.*

This year of *Grace,* by God's especial grace,
When all our foes expected our disgrace,
God crushed their malice, and allay'd our fear:
We *made a happy Change this Present year:*
A Change we made, but yet no Alteration;
Of former happiness a transmigration:
Two froward Sisters long at enmity,
Became the birth-twins of *Virginity,*
From a chaste, virtuous, blessed barren womb,
From the *ill-boding North,* our *Spring* did come;
Whilst many wise foreseeing men did fear,
Who should with quietness be the next *Heir,*
Our fears, so suddenly to joys did pass,
We cannot well tell in what *year* it was.
This year our just victorious *War* did cease,
And we enjoy'd a fought-for proff'red *Peace.*
As soon as our *wise Debora* was gone,
God sent this Land a *Peaceful Salomon.*
Our warlike *Pallas* having rul'd her *days,*

Apollo came, adorn'd with learned Bayes.
Lastly herein our *Chronogram* doth hold,
This year we chang'd our Silver into Gold.
Silver a female is, Gold masculine:
Good *God* lengthen, strengthen this golden Line.
If any wise man judge it otherwise,
I may well judge that Wiseman *overwise.*

7. *Of the Great and Famous, ever to be honoured Knight, Sir* Francis Drake, *and of my little-little self.*

The *Dragon,* that our Seas did raise his Crest,
And brought back heaps of gold unto his nest,
Unto his Foes more terrible than *Thunder,*
Glory of his age, After-ages *wonder,*
Excelling all those that excell'd before;
It's fear'd we shall have none such any more;
Effecting all, he sole did undertake,
Valiant, just, wise, mild, honest, godly *Drake.*
This man when I was little, I did meet,
As he was walking up *Totnes'* long Street,
He ask'd me whose I was? I answer'd him.
He ask'd me if his good friend were within?
A fair red *Orange* in his hand he had,
He gave it me, whereof I was right glad,
Takes and kissed me, and prays, *God bless my boy:*
Which I record *with comfort* to this day.
Could he on me have breathed with his breath,
His gifts *Elias*-like, after his death,
Then had I been enabled for to do
Many brave things I have a heart unto.
I have as great desire, as e'er had *he*
To joy; annoy; friends; foes; but 'twill not be.

8. *To the right Reverend Father in God,* Joseph Hall, *by God's especial providence, Lord Bishop of* Exceter.

Born in a Christian new Plantation,
These kneel to you for Confirmation;

To *you* they come, that *you* might them adorn:
Their Father in your *Diocese* was born.

9. *To the Reverend and divinely witty,* John Dun, *Doctor in Divinity, Dean of Saint* Paul's, London.

As my *John Owen Seneca* did praise,
So might I for you a like pillar raise,
His Epigrams did nothing want but verse;
You can yours (if you list) that way rehearse:
His were neat, fine, divine morality;
But yours, pure, faithful, true Divinity.

10. Aristotle's *ten Predicaments, to be reduced into questions, is an excellent rule for examining any business for matter of justice. To the hopeful and right worthy young Gentleman,* Thomas Smith *of Long-*Ashton *in the County of* Sommerset, *Esq.*

1 2 3

The thing, how much, conditions of the men,

4 5 6

For what cause, what was done, who suffer'd then,

7 8 9 10

Where, when; their postures, how clad, foul, or clean.

11. *Their use.*

Who hath power of examinations,
If he desire to find out guilty ones,
Let him reduce these into questions.
So if to find out truth, be his intent,

Before that all these questions be spent,
The guilty's brought in a Predicament.

12. *The cause of Dedication.*

Strange not, that I these *Lines* to you have sent;
I know, your worth will make you *eminent.*
Grace, Wisdom, Learning, Virtue, you have store;
Were you not modest, I could say much more.

13. *To the Reverend, Learned, and Judicious,* Thomas Worall, *Doctor in Divinity, and Chapalme to the right Rev. Father in God,* George, *L. Bishop of London. Of my reprehending Epigrams.*

It is for one of your gifts, and your place,
To look *bold-staring-black-sin* in the face,
To *wound,* and *lance* with the two-edged blade,
To *cleanse,* and *heal* those wounds that you have made:
Yet suffer me, with my *sharp-merry pin,*
To *prick* the *blisters* of some itching sin.
And though Divines, justly loose Rhymes condemn,
My tart, smart, chiding Lines do not contemn.

14. *To the Reverend, my worthy ingenious friend, Mr.* Abel Lovering, *one of the Preachers of the Word of God at* Bristol. *Of my commending Epigrams.*

Those I commend, you would commend them too,
If you did know them truly, as I do.
Preachers like you, may praise men at their ends,
Laymen like me, may praise wise-living friends.

15. *To a Reverend and witty friend.*

Since few years studying hath improv'd your wit,
That for the place you hold, you are held fit,
When you preach, you preach sweetly and complete,
And other things you do, smooth, witty, neat.

What place in Church would you not fitly hallow;
If you your study soberly would follow?

16. *Of Epigrams.*

Short Epigrams relish both sweet and sour,
Like *Fritters* of sour Apples, and sweet flower.

17. *To the wise and Learned Sir* John Stradling, *Knight Baronet, the Author of divers Divine Heroicall printed Poems.*

Robert Fitz-Heman drew your Ancestor
To *Wales,* to be his fellow Conqueror.
And *Robert Hayman* would draw all your worth,
If he true knowledge had, to limb it forth.
Wise Sir, I know you not, but by relation,
Saving in this, which spreads your reputation:
Your high divine sweet strains *Poetical.*
Which crowns, adorns your noble virtues all.
Therein to dight a full Feast, you are able,
Whilst I fit Fritters for *Apollo's* Table.

18. *To Master* Benjamin Johnson, *Witty Epigrammatist, and most excellent Poet.*

My Epigrams come after yours in time;
So do they in conceit, in form, in Rhyme;
My *wit's* in fault, the fault is none of mine:
For if my *will* could have inspir'd my *wit,*
There never had been better Verses writ,
As good as *yours,* could I have ruled it.

19. *To one of my neat Readers.*

Thou say'st, my are Verses rude, ragged, rough,
Not like some others Rhymes, smooth, dainty stuff.
Epigrams are like *Satires,* rough without,
Like *Chestnuts,* sweet, take thou the kernel out.
Satires.

20. *To the acute Satirist, Master* George Wither.

> The *efficient cause* of *Satires,* are things bad,
> Their *matter,* sharp reproofs, instructions sad,
> Their *form* sour, short, severe, sharp, roughly clad:
> Their *end* is that *amendment* may be had.

21. *To the same Mr.* George Wither, *of his own Satires.*

> What cause you had, this vein too high to strain,
> I know not, but I know, it caus'd your pain;
> Which causeth others wisely to refrain:
> Yet let some good cause draw you on again.
> You strip and whip th'ill *manners* of the times
> So handsomely, that all delight your Rhymes.

22. *To my right worthy friend, Mr.* Michael Drayton, *whose unwearied old Muse still produceth dainties.*

> When I was young, I did *delight* your lines,
> I have *admir'd* them since my judging times:
> Your *younger muse* play'd many a dainty fit,
> And your *old muse* doth hold out stoutly yet.
> Though my *old muse* durst pass through frost and snow,
> In wars your *old muse* dares her Colours show.

23. *To my worthy and learned good friend, Mr.* John Vicars, *who hath translated part of Mr.* Owens *Epigrams.*

> Who hath good words, and a warm brooding pate,
> Shall easier hatch neat new things, than translate:
> He that translates, must walk as others please:
> Writing our own, we wander may at ease.

24. *To my good friend, Mr.* T.B. *Vintner, at the sign of the Sun in* Milke-street.

> *Bacchus* desiring an auspicious sign,

Under which he might sell his choicest *wine,*
Desiring much to choose one of the seven
Celestial Planets, reel'd one night to heaven,
He found old Bent-brow'd *Saturn* melancholly,
Jove stern, *Mars* stout, *Venus* replete with folly,
Sly *Mercury* full of Loquacity,
And *Luna* troubled with inconstancy:

Disliking these, he *middle Sol* espied,
Who unto *sober drinkers* is a guide:
He liking this, in *via Lactea* placed it,
And with his *best wines,* he hath e'er since graced it,
And finding you no *Brewer,* as your due,
He doth commit the charge thereof to *You.*

27. *To a Friend, who asked me why I do not compose some particular Epigrams to our most gracious King, as my Friend* John Owen *did to his famous Father, King* JAMES of *blessed memory.*

Thou ask'st, Why I do not spin out my wit,
In silken threads, and fine, smooth, neat lines fit,
In special *Epigrams* to our wise King?
All these myself I dedicate to him.
It's all too coarse, what my wit can weave forth,
To wrap the little finger of his worth.

28. *Sin's short Grammar.*
To my loving Cousin Master John Gunning *the younger, of Bristol Merchant.*

The Grammar.
Sin's easy *Grammar,* our Grandmother *Eve*
To her sinful posterity did *leave.*
Sin's Part.
In *Speach* are eight parts, in sin there are seven,
We may put *Satan* in, to make them even.
Satan a Noun.

Satan, Sin's grandfather, stands as a *Noun,*
To all ill things giving an ill renown,
Enticing mildly; Roaring if withstood.
Being thereby *felt, heard, and understood.*

Sloth, a Pronoun.

Sloth is a *Pronoun:* Idle men in name
Are men, but otherwise a senseless shame.
Sloth is the *Deuil's* best son *Primitive,*
And from him most sins do themselves *derive.*

Anger, A Verb.

Anger a Verb is, for at every word,
His *Active* and his *Passive* spleen is stir'd,
In *Mood* and *Tense* declined is this sin,
Moody it is, at all times full of spleen.

Covetousness, a Participle.

Covetousness may be sin's *participle,*
To help himself, from each one takes a little,
With every *Sin* he will *Participate,*
So he thereby may better his estate.

Pride, an Adverb.

Pride is an *Aduerb,* if you'll take his word,
Nor Heaven, nor Earth the like thing doth afford.
In his conceit he is the thing alone,
He holds himself beyond *Comparison.*

Lust, a Conjunction.

Lust is a lawless, lewd *Conjunction,*
For *Lust* desires not to act sin alone:
So *joining* sins his sinful days dost waste,
Until they join him with the *Deuil* at last.

Envy, a Preposition.

Envy may be Sin's *Preposition,*
'Gainst things well compos'd showing opposition.
Ablatives, and *Accusatives* he'll choose
For he loves to *Detract,* and to *Accuse.*

Gluttony, an Interjection.

Gluttony is an Interjection,
Into his paunch all his delights are thrown.

As nothing but *good bits,* can make him glad,
So only want of them, can make him sad.

Sin's Declension.

O God! in what bad *Case* are we *declin'd?*
Since thou in every *Case* our sins maist find,
In *Nominative,* by furious Appellations,
In *Genitive,* by spurious generations.
In *Dative,* by corrupting bribery.
In the *Accusative,* by calumny.
In *Vocative,* by grudging, and exclaiming.
In *Ablative,* by coz'ning, rape, and stealing.

Number, and Gender.

Singular sins, and *Plural* we commit,
And we in every *Gender* vary it.

Number.

Our *Single* sins are wicked cogitations,
Our *Plural,* Riots, Combinations
Against thee, *Lord,* and thy *Anointed* ones.

Gender.

Out *Masculine,* first sin's uxoriousness,
Our *Feminine,* to sin's sleights yieldingness,
Our *Neuter* sin, is cold neutrality,
Common of two, too common Venery.
Thrice Common we commit sins against *Three;*
Against our selves, our Neighbours, against *Thee.*
Doubtful is our Dissimulation.
In all sins, *Hes* and *Shes* take delectation.

The Conclusion.

Thus we in Sin use regularility,
Whil'st *We* with *Grace* have no Congruity.

29. *To lashing, fault-finding Zoilus.*

I know, thou wilt end, as thou hast begun:
Put up thy Rod (great whipper) I have done.

30. *To the ineffable, individual, ever blessed Trinity in Unity.*

To one in *three, three* in one be all praise,
For planting in me, this small bud of *Bays.*

The end of the Author's *Quodlibets.* At this time.

To the Reader, instead of an Epistle.

If these fail in worth, blame me, but consider from whence they came; from a place of no helps. If in Printing, blame the Printer, and mend it. I have omitted many of mine own and of the Translations. As thou likest these, thou maist have the rest.

FAREWELL.

CERTAIN

EPIGRAMS OUT

OF THE FIRST FOUR

BOOKS OF THE EXCELLENT EPIGRAMMATIST,

MASTER JOHN OWEN:

TRANSLATED INTO ENGLISH
AT HARBOR-GRACE IN
Bristol's-Hope in Britaniola,
anciently called New-found-land:

By R.H.

AT LONDON

Imprinted for Roger Michell,
and are to be sold at
the sign of the Bull's head
in Paul's Churchyard. 1628.

TO THE FAR ADMIRED, ADMIRABLLY FAIR,
virtuous, and witty Beauties of
ENGLAND.

IT was, fair, virtuous, witty, for your sake,
That I this harder task did undertake.
I griev'd, such was out of your command,
Lock'd in a tongue you did not understand.
To do you service, not myself to please,
Did I at first adventure upon these.

I thought to have proceeded in this method, but the ragged, bashful flat my Muse (having not seen your like before) is amazed, and stricken dumb at the sight of your excellencies: I must therefore take up the speech for her, and as She hath heretofore twaddled much for me, I must therefore entreat you in Her behalf. Indeed I told Her, She should find you very loving and kind, and should be admitted to kiss your whitest hands. She is a stranger, I humbly therefore pray you, to take her into your protection, kindly take her into your hands, and entertain her courteously; none can do it better then yourselves; whilst you look kindly upon her, let her with admiration, and contentment gaze on your beauties: you may look upon her boldly with unveiled countenances, you shall find her every where modest, either she hath veiled, or quite omitted what She fears might offend your chaste ears, She hath taken pains to let you know what envious me have too long kept from your knowledge. If She speak any thing against your sex, it is but what malicious men sometimes mutter in an unknown language against your inferior frailties, and hath answered somewhat in your behalf: you shall find Her no importunate Companion, for you may begin with her when you please, and leave her when you list: every small parcel is an entire treatise, and depends upon itself; they may serve you for pastime, if you please, for use, for embellishing in your discourse, as spangles in your attire: The translations were the better, if they are not made worse in the change. For our own, they are the best we can at this time. The grace and love I received sometime from one of your sex, makes me confident of your gracious goodness: but my Muse hath a little recovered her spirits, and requests me She may speak a little unto you.

Your beauties, wonder and amazement bred
In me, that still I am astonished:
Yet this request I pray do not deny,
Give me good words, for you have more than I.
In recompense one day I'll sing a song
Of your rich worth with my last buskins on.

The admirer of your excellencies,
the short-breath'd Muse of
Robert Hayman.

A PREMONITION TO ALL KIND OF READERS of these Translations of John Owen's EPIGRAMS.

As one into a spacious Garden led,
Which is with rare, fair flowers well garnished,
Where Argus may all his eyes satisfy;
Centimanus all his hands occupy,
He will choose some fine flowers of the best,
To make himself a Poesy at the least:
Or he will, if such favour may be found,
Entreat some Slips, to set in his own ground:
So fares it with me, when in Owen's book,
At leisure times, with willing eyes I look:
I cannot choose, but choose some of his flowers,
And to translate them at my leisure hours.
But as 'tis not for this admitted Man,
Manners at once to gather every one,
But mildly to cull a few at a time,
I pray thee do so too, kind Reader mine:
For as a Man may surfeit on sweet meats:
So thou maist over-read these quaint conceits.
Some at one time, some at another choose;
As Maidens do their kissing Conceits use.
Read therefore these, His; by translation, Mine:
As some eat Cheese, a penny-weight at a time.

AN ENCOMIASTICK DISTICK ON MY RIGHT WORTHY AUTHOR, JOHN OWEN.

The best conceits Owen's conceits have found,
Short, sharp, sweet, witty, unforc'd, neat, profound.

SEVERAL SENTENTIOUS EPIGRAMS, AND WITTY SAYINGS OUT
of sundry Authors both Ancient and Modern:

TRANSLATED INTO ENGLISH AT HARBOR-Grace, in Bristol's-Hope, in Britaniola,

Anciently called, New-found-land;

By R.H.

LONDON,
Printed by Felix Kingston for Roger Michell,
and are to be sold at the Bull's-head in Paul's
Church-yard. 1628.

A WEAK APOLOGY FOR MY WEAKENESS
in these following Translations.

We think it no strange thing; nor do we laugh,
To see and old, weak man walk with a staff:
I that could with strong legs run a large fit,
Must now with short turns, rest on others' wit.

SELECTED BIBLIOGRAPHY

Hayman, Robert. *Quodlibets, lately come over from New Britaniola, old Newfoundland.* Roger Mitchell: London. 1628.

Hayman, Robert and G. C. Moore Smith. "Robert Hayman and the Plantation of Newfoundland." *The English Historical Review*, Vol. 34, No. 129 (Jan. 1918). Oxford University Press. 21-36.

Hearnshaw, F. J. C. "The Death of Robert Hayman, November 1629." *The English Historical Review*, Vol. 34, No. 136 (Oct. 1919). Oxford University Press. 590-591.

PROBLEMATIC
PRESS

www.ingramcontent.com/pod-product-compliance
Lightning Source LLC
LaVergne TN
LVHW010937110826
845149LV00013B/2634

* 9 7 8 0 9 8 6 9 0 2 7 2 7 *